MAKE YOUR OWN

¡Salsa!

Author/Editor: Cindy Burda
Art and production: Thomas Gaines
Assistant editor: Catharine Sutherland
Editorial assistant: Heather Smith

Library of Congress Cataloging-in-Publication Data
Burda, Cindy, 1972–
    Make Your Own ¡Salsa! / Cindy Burda. — 1st ed.
      p.   cm.
    Includes index.
    ISBN 1-57990-123-9 (pbk.)
    1. Salsas (Cookery)   I. Title
    TX819.S29B87 1999
    641.8'14—dc21   98-53005
                                                  CIP

10 9 8 7 6 5 4 3 2 1

First Edition

Published by Lark Books
50 College St.
Asheville, NC 28801, USA

© 1998, Lark Books

Distributed by Random House, Inc., in the United States and Canada.

The written instructions, designs, and recipes in this volume are intended for the personal use of the reader and may be reproduced for that purpose only. Any other use, especially commercial use, is forbidden under law without written permission of the copyright holder.

Every effort has been made to ensure that all the information in this book is accurate. However, due to differing conditions, tools, and individual skills, the publisher cannot be responsible for any injuries, losses, or other damages that may result from the use of the information in this book.

Printed in China
All rights reserved.
ISBN 1-57990-123-9

▼

MAKE YOUR OWN

¡Salsa!

CINDY BURDA

Contents

6 Introduction

8 Tools, Techniques, and One Lonely Tip

11 Some Common Salsa Ingredients

17 A (Somewhat) Definitive Guide to Chilies

23 The Recipes

62 Acknowledgments

63 Index to Recipes

64 Index to Subjects

Introduction

One recent day, as I was rhapsodizing about salsas, a friend of mine said to me, "What's the big deal, anyway? Salsas are pretty much all the same, aren't they?" I gasped, horrified that any acquaintance of mine could have so little salsa savvy. "Oh no, my friend! Salsas are not at all 'all the same.'" To prove my point, I opened my refrigerator and whipped out a bowl of a magnificent pineapple-chipotle creation I'd diced into existence the day before. I offered him the bowl and a bag of tortilla chips. "Try this. Then tell me that all salsas are the same."

Needless to say, the experience changed his life. He immediately quit his job as a computer consultant, moved to the Caribbean, and is now whiling away his days as the owner of an exotic dance club. Actually, that's not what happened, but it sounds good, doesn't it? What really happened was that, after demolishing the entire bag of chips and all my pineapple-chipotle salsa, he asked for a beer. Then he demanded the recipe. I gladly shared it with him, and although he doesn't actually live in the Caribbean, he claims that every time he whips up a batch of that hot, sweet wonder, the taste transports him to the tropics. His blood pressure is down, his love-life is up, and he's found new joy in living. (If you're interested, you'll find the recipe for that very same salsa on page 52.)

My point is this: If the only salsas you've ever tried are the ones that come pre-packaged in a bottle from your grocery store, you—like my friend—are in for some very tasty surprises. Start with traditional salsas—blends of fresh tomatoes, peppers, and onions. These simple mixtures burst with bright flavor, and they can be endlessly varied with subtle spices and additional ingredients. Then move on to today's cutting-edge recipes—delicious creations that stretch the basic concept of salsa far beyond its humble roots. Contemporary salsas incorporate a huge array of ingredients, from exotic and everyday fruits to sesame seeds and spices. Some salsas are fiery hot—so thick with serranos and jalapeños that only the most devout chile-heads can enjoy them. Others are packed with flavor—but boast not a lick of flame.

This book includes recipes from both ends of the heat spectrum, and many from in between, as well. No matter what your heat preference—hot as Hades or mild as the morning dew on springtime grass—you'll find plenty of salsas to please your palate. I should know—I've risked mine experimenting with the recipes in this book!

And from that experimentation, I've discovered that the perfect salsa isn't defined by its ingredients, but by how those ingredients taste together. The recipes in this book will give you a great start on figuring out which ingredients belong with one another. After you get a feel (or taste) for flavors that work well together, you'll be ready to create your own signature recipes. Add chilies if you want more heat; leave them out if you want less. Try your favorite herbs in place of the ones suggested. Raid your garden for new ingredients. You're going to have a great time with this! So good luck, have fun—and feel free to send samples of your successes.

Tools, Techniques, and One Lonely Tip

I'm not kidding when I say that making good—even great—salsa is easy. We're talking about chopping up fruit and vegetables here—maybe adding a few spices and roasting some chili peppers. Nevertheless, there are some tools and techniques that make the job even easier.

Tools

BLENDER OR FOOD PROCESSOR
Not all salsas are thick and chunky—you'll grind some to a smooth paste. You can accomplish this with grinding stones (the traditional method), or you can do it with a blender or food processor. I usually go for one of the latter two.

CUTTING BOARD
Making salsa involves a lot of cutting, chopping, mincing, and dicing. A cutting board makes all of these much easier.

LABELS AND GLASS JARS OR BOTTLES
It's not a bad idea to dedicate a few glass jars or bottles to your salsa-making adventures. As you fill each jar with a new concoction, simply stick a label on it indicating the contents and date of production. Doing so will ensure that you always know what's what in your refrigerator (or at least what's salsa and what's not), which will help you avoid the common mistake of spooning minced maraschino cherries over your midnight snack of cheddar cheese and jalapeño nachos.

GRATER
Several of the following recipes call for fresh, grated ginger—hence the need for a grater.

HERB CHOPPER

One of the keys to well-made salsa is cutting the individual ingredients to an appropriate size. Herbs are usually minced finely, and an herb chopper is the preferred tool for this job.

LEMON REAMER

Lemon or lime juice can add just the zing a salsa needs to be truly exceptional. Fresh juice always tastes better than processed, and a reamer will allow you to enjoy the freshest juice possible.

POTS AND PANS

You won't need many cooking implements for making salsas because you won't be doing much cooking. However, a few recipes require a medium-size pot for boiling water, or a medium-size frying pan for toasting ingredients. In general, heavy-bottomed pots and pans work best for any kind of cooking because they distribute heat evenly.

THIN SURGICAL RUBBER GLOVES

Rubber gloves aren't exactly common kitchen implements, but if you're going to be handling many hot chilies (and if you want your salsa to sizzle, you will be), your tender hands will thank you for protecting them.

Techniques

SKINNING TOMATOES

Some people don't mind tomato skins in their salsas, and other people do. Either way, getting rid of tomato skins is a snap. Start by boiling enough water to submerge all the tomatoes you want to peel. Carefully add the tomatoes to the boiling water and cook for about 30 seconds. Use a slotted spoon to transfer the fruit to a bowl of ice water. Soak for about 20 seconds; then make a small incision in each tomato and use your hands to remove the skins—they should slip right off.

PEELING ONIONS

Most varieties of onions arrive in your kitchen covered in several layers of thin, papery skin that should be removed before use. Here's how to make the task easier: Submerge the onions in boiling water for 2 to 3 minutes; then drain and place them in very cold water for 1 minute. The skins will peel easily away.

ROASTING CHILIES

Several recipes in this book call for roasting chilies before use. Once you taste the delicious, smoky result of this process, you may want to include roasted chilies in other recipes, too. Here's how to do it: Arrange the whole chilies on a baking sheet lined with aluminum foil. Use a fork or sharp knife to pierce several holes in each one; then place the baking sheet in the oven about 4 to 6 inches from the broiler. Turn the oven to broil and cook until the chilies are charred and wrinkled on all sides; you'll need to flip them once or twice to make sure that every inch gets roasted. You'll also want to keep a close eye on them to make sure they don't burn. Seal the charred chilies in a paper bag for 20 minutes to "steam" their skins loose. Remove the stems, seeds, and membranes; then pull off the skins. Voila—roasted chilies ready for use in your favorite recipe.

And One Lonely Tip

My single tip to you is simply this: Read the recipe. Read it all the way through before you even begin to *think* about chopping a single tomato. Check your refrigerator, your vegetable basket, and your kitchen shelves to make sure that you have all the required ingredients (or suitable substitutes) on hand. Nothing's more frustrating than getting your taste buds all excited for a late-night helping of Roasted Habañero Salsa (page 40), only to find that you're fresh out of habañeros, with no way to get more.

Some Common Salsa Ingredients

I'd bet money (not my own, of course, but money nevertheless) that even those of you whose knowledge of cooking begins with TV dinners and ends at the control panel of your microwave will have at least a nodding acquaintance with most of the ingredients that turn up in this book. After all, great salsas aren't about exotic ingredients—they're about exotic combinations of ingredients. That said, keep in mind that your salsa will only be as good as its individual components, so use top-quality, fresh produce whenever possible. This section will give you the information you need to select the best ingredients available.

AVOCADOES

Most grocery stores carry two kinds of avocadoes: Fuerte and Haas. Fuerte avocadoes are the ones with slick, green skins. Haas avocadoes have dark, pebbly-textured skins that turn black when the fruits ripen. Use Haas avocadoes if you can find them; ripe, they have a creamy, buttery flesh that's perfect in salsas. If you can't find ripe avocadoes, storing the unripened fruits in a paper bag at room temperature for 2 or 3 days will speed ripening.

CHILIES

There's only one really good way to give your salsa some sear, and that's voodoo. I jest, of course—chilies are the preferred method. These (sometimes) fiery fruits are so important to salsa making that they rate their very own section in this book; that section starts on page 17.

CILANTRO (A.K.A. CORIANDER)

Cilantro is an "either-or" kind of herb: Either you really love it, or you really hate it. Those who love it wouldn't dream of making salsa without it, and personally, I'd use cilantro-flavored dental floss if such a thing existed. If you fall into the "really hate it" camp, simply omit the herb from any recipe that calls for it.

You'll find fresh cilantro in the produce section of your grocery store, probably near its close cousin, parsley. Use the leaves and tender upper stems and refrigerate any leftovers in a mug of cold water covered with a plastic bag. One bunch of cilantro yields about ¾ to 1 cup when chopped.

CORIANDER SEEDS

These are the seeds from which cilantro plants spring. Ground coriander seeds have a completely different taste from fresh cilantro, so even if you hate the herb cilantro, you may love the spice coriander.

CUCUMBERS

These darlings of the summer vegetable garden add great crunch and texture to many salsas. Small pickling cucumbers are the best choice; they have a much firmer, less sweet (but not bitter) flesh than their larger counterparts. Although the recipes in this book call for peeling the cucumbers, unless they're waxed, peeling isn't a necessary step. In fact, I like the added color and texture that unpeeled cukes add to a salsa.

CUMIN

This rich, almost meaty-tasting spice is a hallmark of Mexican cooking. You'll always use ground rather than whole, cumin in salsas, so either buy the spice ground, or grind the whole spice yourself in a spice grinder or coffee grinder. If you find that you've included one (or eight) too many chilies in your salsa, try adding a little extra cumin; in addition to tasting great, it can help cool an overly-fiery concoction.

GARLIC

All-healing, vampire-defying, and an absolute must for a good number of salsa recipes, you'll want to buy garlic fresh by the head. A head consists of several cloves that should be peeled before chopping. As a general rule, the larger the head (and its cloves), the milder and better the flavor.

GINGER

Make a sincere effort to find fresh ginger—it has a spicy, fresh aroma and flavor that the dried powder just can't match. Plus, you'll sound really professional when you refer to a fresh ginger root as a "hand," as in, "Honey, if you really want to help, grate about 2 tablespoons of that hand of ginger." Sounds pretty gourmet, doesn't it? And as long as your honey is willing to help out, be sure that he or she peels the ginger before grating it. It's so nice to have help in the kitchen, isn't it?

JÍCAMA

Pronounced "HEE-kah-mah," this root vegetable is sometimes called the Mexican potato. It has a nutty-tasting, sweet, white flesh that has the same texture as a water chestnut. Peel the jícama's thin skin just before use. You'll find this vegetable in Latin markets and most well-stocked grocery stores.

LEMONS AND LIMES

Many salsas just wouldn't be the same without a good tart note tying together all the other flavors; lemon or lime juice is perfect for adding this essential tang. I highly recommend buying whole lemons and limes and squeezing the juice fresh—just be sure to rinse the fruits well before cutting into them.

MANGOES

If you've never tried one of these delicious tropical fruits, the time has definitely come! The sweet, very orange, and slightly tart flesh of a ripe mango is the perfect foil for searing hot chilies, and the combination results in truly transcendental salsas. Mangoes are readily available in well-stocked grocery stores between May and September (when the fruit is in season), and somewhat less readily available in health-food stores and specialty markets the rest of the year. The recipes in this book call for ripe mangoes. You can identify a ripe mango by its yellow skin mottled with red patches. If you can't find ripe mangoes, try the trick suggested on page 11 for ripening avocadoes.

MEXICAN OREGANO

Because Mexican oregano has a stronger, more intense flavor than its European cousin, it's a perfect spice for salsas; it simply refuses to be overwhelmed by garlic, onions, chilies, and other robust ingredients. You'll find this spice in Latin markets, and it's also increasingly available at many grocery stores. It's almost always sold dried, and should be crumbled before use. If you can't find Mexican oregano, use ordinary oregano instead—simply increase the amount to reach the desired flavor.

ONIONS

It is the rare salsa recipe indeed that does not call for an onion of some variety—and there are plenty of varieties from which to choose. Substituting one kind of onion for another is a great way to vary the flavor of a salsa, and you should definitely do some experimenting to discover what kinds you like. Keep in mind that red onions (including red Italian, Bermuda, and purple onions) are generally quite sweet and mild. Yellow Vidalia and Spanish onions are also sweet and mild, while yellow globe onions are much stronger and more pungent. White globe onions are stronger still. Green onions (or scallions) are also quite strong; for a more delicate flavor, use chives instead. Now, go forth and select onions with confidence!

PEPPERCORN

Do yourself—and your taste buds—a favor: invest in a pepper mill and several ounces of whole peppercorn. Intense, rich, and nothing at all like the tasteless grey powder that lurks on dining-room tables across the country, freshly ground peppercorn is a culinary epiphany, a fiesta for the senses, and an essential for great salsas.

PINEAPPLE

You won't believe how good fresh pineapple tastes in salsa! It's actually quite easy to work with, too. Simply twist off the pineapple's leafy top (a good, ripe pineapple's top will twist right off). Then remove and discard the pineapple skin. The easiest way to do this is to stand the pineapple upright, and using a sharp kitchen knife, slice away the skin in vertical strips, moving from top to bottom. Cut the peeled pineapple in quarters, lengthwise; then cut out and discard the hard core. That's it. If you must, you may substitute canned pineapple; just be sure to drain it well first.

SESAME SEEDS

These small, plump, ivory-colored seeds have a wonderful nutty flavor that can enhance just about any recipe. They're especially nice in salsas because, in addition to good flavor, they also add an excellent texture, completely different from any other salsa ingredient.

TOMATILLOS

As their name suggests, tomatillos are closely related to tomatoes. In fact, they look like nothing so much as small green versions of their more familiar cousins. Ripe tomatillos are yellow, but most recipes—including the ones in this book—call for the fruits in their unripened, green state. You'll find tomatillos in Latin markets, health-food stores, and well-stocked supermarkets. They generally come wrapped in their natural papery husks, which should be removed before use. If you can't find tomatillos, green tomatoes make a reasonable substitute; use 1 medium-size tomato for every 3 tomatillos.

TOMATOES

As every gardener knows, vine-ripened tomatoes are infinitely superior to the pale fruit that languishes in the produce section of your local grocery store; however, if those sad, pallid tomatoes are the only ones to which you have access, setting them on a sunny windowsill for a day or two will do wonders for their looks and flavor.

Gardeners also know that there are plenty of varieties of tomatoes from which to select. In general, firm, ripe fruit of a medium size is a good choice for most salsas. The best choice of all, however, is probably the plum (or Roma) tomato; this is a small, very firm fruit that's less juicy than most other kinds. It also has a very thin skin. Some folks claim that tomato skins can spoil the texture of a salsa, so they peel the tomatoes before using them. Personally, I like the added texture and almost never peel my tomatoes, but if you'd like to learn how, turn to page 9. With plum tomatoes, even picky people can skip the peeling bit. Most of the recipes in this book don't specify a particular variety of tomato and assume a medium to large fruit; if you'd like to use plum tomatoes instead, substitute 2 to 3 plums for every 1 ordinary tomato.

A (Somewhat) Definitive Guide to Chilies

For some folks, salsa isn't salsa unless it induces prolific sweating on a January day in Minnesota. It was for these people that Mother Nature created hot chili peppers. Fortunately, she kept the rest of us in mind, too, and we have a huge selection of chilies from which to choose—including many very flavorful, but non-incendiary varieties. In other words: Don't shy away from a salsa recipe just because you're not a full-blown chilehead. You can leave chilies out, substitute mild chilies for hot ones, or add as many chilies as it takes to make smoke curl from your ears—the choice is yours. But chilies do add great flavor to salsas, and if you like heat, they can add that, too. Take a minute to learn about these fun little fruits, try a few out, and you'll soon be adding them to everything you cook.

A Glossary of Common Chili Peppers

Chilies can be confusing. They turn colors, they switch names, and they refuse to maintain a predictable level of heat—even within the same species. That green chili pepper you know and love as a poblano may be masquerading, dried and red, as an ancho. The searing jalapeño that scorched your tongue today may have grown just one row over from the jalapeño that you consumed raw last week without batting an eye. To add to the confusion, people in different places often call the same chilies by different names. And even your grocer might not know exactly what's what when it comes to chilies—you'll sometimes find peppers mislabeled in even the very finest of produce sections. But before you throw in your hat and give up on ever figuring out the bewildering world of the chili pepper, look over the following glossary—it's not foolproof, but it will help you sort through the myriad of commonly available chilies.

Not every chili mentioned here shows up in the recipes that follow, but you'll want to know about them anyway in case you need to substitute what you have on hand for what's listed in the recipe. As long as you keep an eye on the heat, you can usually substitute one green chili for another or one dried chili for another. The chilies are listed in approximate order of escalating hotness, but keep in mind that the peppers you take home will have their own personalities.

ANAHEIM (a.k.a *California*)

This mild chili has only slightly more heat than a bell pepper, and it looks a little like one, too—just longer and thinner. At 5 to 7 inches long, it's one of the largest chilies around. Fresh Anaheims are usually sold green, but they turn bright red when left to mature. The mature red chilies are often dried, and although they look completely different from the fresh peppers, they're also called Anaheims.

NEW MEXICO (*chile de ristra, Chimayo, Hatch, Dixon*)

This is a hotter and more flavorful cousin of the Anaheim chile. It shares its size and shape with its relative, but the fresh New Mexico is usually sold mature when it's deep red in color. It's also sold dried, strung in garlands called "ristras." Chimayo, Hatch, and Dixon are all types of New Mexico chilies, each with its own flavor.

FRESNO

This fairly mild, 2- to 3-inch long chili is generally sold red.

ANCHO

See poblano.

POBLANO

This dark green, triangular-shaped chili is usually about 3 to 5 inches long and 2 to 3 inches wide at its stem. It's generally a moderately hot pepper, but the heat varies widely from chili to chili. If you're using fresh poblanos, you may want to remove their tough skins first. Dried poblanos are called anchos and have a dark reddish color and smoky flavor.

MULATO
This is a slightly larger version of the poblano.

PASILLA *(a.k.a. Chile negro, black chili)*
Pasillas are harvested when they're very dark in color. Dried, they're purple-black in color and 5 to 7 inches long. They have an intense, spicy flavor, and are hotter and less sweet than anchos.

CHIPOTLE
See jalapeño.

JALAPEÑO
The most familiar and easy-to-find chili north of the Mexican border, the jalapeño is 2 to 4 inches long, with a sharp flavor, medium to hot heat, and a long, intense burn. Fresh jalapeños are generally sold when they're bright green. Dried, smoked jalapeños are known as chipotles and are often packed in a piquant, red sauce called adobo. Fresh jalapeños may be used as substitutes for hotter chili peppers—just use more.

GUAJILLO
See mirasol.

MIRASOL
This medium-hot, medium-size pepper is long and tapered. It's often seen strung in "ristras" (garlands) to dry. Dried mirasols are called guajillos. They have a fruity flavor, a brownish-orange color, and a heat index that ranges from medium to very hot.

BANANA PEPPER
This medium-hot chili is normally sold fresh when it's yellow or yellow-green, and that's where the name comes from. Banana peppers can range in size from 1 to 5 inches long, and are often mistaken for the much hotter Hungarian hot wax pepper—even by grocers, so watch your step in the produce bin.

CHILE DE ARBOL
This pepper is usually sold in powdered form and is fairly hot. When whole, the dried fruit is long and very thin. It's usually dried when it's bright orange-red.

CAYENNE
This is a thin, tapered, hot red chili. It usually appears in the form of a ground powder, but whole cayennes (fresh or dried) are quite good, too. Fresh cayennes may be used in place of jalapeños, habañeros, and serranos.

SERRANO
The serrano is a slightly smaller, hotter version of the jalapeño.

PIQUIN
This is a tiny, hot-as-heck red chili that's used primarily in commercial hot pepper sauces. Piquins are also available both fresh and dried at some grocery stores and most Latin markets. These chilies are a little on the pricey side, but you get a lot of bang for your buck.

TEPIN
This chili is closely related and similar to the piquin.

TABASCO
The Tabasco pepper is very hot and must be handled with care. Like the piquin, most Tabasco peppers are grown for use in commercial hot pepper sauces, although you will occasionally find them fresh or dried.

HABAÑERO (*a.k.a. Scotch Bonnet*)
This chili's lantern shape makes it look a little like a small, walnut-sized bell pepper, but that's where the resemblance ends. Habañeros, which range in color from green to bright orange, are generally considered to be the hottest chilies commercially available; their oil can actually blister skin. Despite their dangerous heat, habañeros have a wonderful flavor—just be careful with them!

Handling Chilies

The watch word here is careful. I recommend wearing thin surgical gloves (available at most pharmacies) whenever you work with hot peppers—your skin will thank you. Always wash your hands with soap and water after handling any kind of chili, and never, ever touch your eyes if there's even a remote possibility that any chili residue remains on your hands. Most of a chili's heat comes from its seeds and inner white membranes; removing these will tame a lot of the chili's flame. When you're done, scrub down all the surfaces and utensils that came in contact with the fiery fruits.

Storing Chilies

Dried chilies will keep for several months when stored in a sealed plastic bag in the refrigerator. Keep powdered chilies flavorful by storing them in tightly closed bottles or jars tucked into a dark cupboard. Wrap fresh chilies individually in paper towels and store them in the refrigerator where they'll keep for up to 1 week.

Taming the Flame

Let's say you've scorched your tongue with a wickedly hot habañero (or any other hot chili, for that matter). Your first instinct may be to stick your head under the nearest tap, be it for water or beer. In this case, your first instinct is wrong. Capsicum, the active ingredient that gives chilies their burn-power, is oil-based, and water won't do a thing to rinse it away. Dairy products are what you need to soothe a seared tongue. Milk, yogurt, cheese, sour cream, and—yes!—ice cream will all do the trick.

the recipes

For many folks, salsa means one thing and one thing only: A chunky tomato sauce with onions, garlic, and maybe a few chilies thrown in for good measure. And there's certainly nothing wrong with that combination! For other folks, though, salsa has come to mean any of a huge range of innovative, interesting, and delicious blends of fruits, vegetables, herbs, and spices. I scoured my own recipe files, hit up my friends and family, and generally searched near and far to compile a collection of salsa recipes that would give you a taste of everything out there—from basic, traditional blends to the most cutting-edge concoctions assembled to date. But don't think for a minute that all the great salsas have already been created. Use your imagination. Pick a recipe that sounds good and try it out. Add ingredients that you like. Leave out ingredients that you don't like. Take notes. Share with friends. Above all, have a good time! Soon you'll have your own great collection of personalized salsa recipes. So what are you waiting for? Get to it!

Your Basic Salsa

You won't find any of those highfalutin herbs and spices in this recipe. No fancy-schmancy tropical fruits, either. No sir; no ma'am. Just your most basic, traditional salsa ingredients. You got your tomatoes, your onion, a couple of chilies, some garlic, and a little salt. What else do you need, anyway? Chopped coarsely, this is one fine chip-dipping salsa. Run it through a blender, simmer it for a few minutes, and you've got yourself a classy alternative to ketchup.

MAKES ABOUT 1 ¼ CUPS

- 2 large tomatoes
- 1 small yellow onion, peeled
- 2 serrano chilies
- 2 cloves garlic, peeled
- ¼ teaspoon salt or to taste

Cut the tomatoes into quarters, and remove and discard the seeds. Chop the tomatoes into ¼-inch cubes. Dice the onion finely. Remove and discard the seeds and membranes from the serrano chilies. Chop the chilies finely. Mince the garlic. Combine all the ingredients and serve immediately. Leftovers will keep in the refrigerator for 2 to 3 days, but freshness is this salsa's hallmark. Besides, you'll probably eat it all in one sitting, anyway.

For that classy ketchup alternative mentioned earlier, process this salsa in a blender until smooth, but not liquified. In a large frying pan over high heat, warm 2 tablespoons of vegetable oil. Add the blended salsa and stir constantly for 5 minutes. Remove from the heat and serve when the salsa has cooled to room temperature. Store in the refrigerator for up to 1 week.

Salsa Cruda

Want a classic salsa? This is it. Salsa Cruda is one of the most basic, all-purpose salsas around. Serve it with any kind of grilled meat, pile it on a homemade pizza, fold it into an omelet, or just dip some tortilla chips in it. If you're a salsa purist, you're going to love this one. Heck, even if you're not, you'll love it anyway.

MAKES ABOUT 2 CUPS

- 2 large, very ripe tomatoes
- 1 medium white onion, peeled
- 2 green onions
- 1 jalapeño chili
- 1 serrano chili
- 2 tablespoons fresh cilantro, chopped
- 2 teaspoons fresh lime juice
- 1/8 teaspoon ground cumin
- 1/8 teaspoon Mexican oregano
- 1/2 teaspoon salt or to taste

Cut the tomatoes into quarters, remove and discard their seeds, and chop the tomatoes coarsely (¼- to ½-inch cubes are a good size). Chop the onion to the same size as the tomatoes. Remove and discard the seeds and membranes from the chilies, and chop the chilies to about half the size of the tomatoes and onions. Place all the ingredients in a bowl, toss to blend well, and serve immediately. Store any leftovers in the refrigerator for up to 2 days.

Pico de Gallo Salsa

"Pico de Gallo" means "beak of the rooster" in Spanish. Don't worry, though. As you look over the list of ingredients, you'll note that this recipe calls for nary a beak, rooster or otherwise (which isn't to say that you can't add a few, if you really want). The name actually refers to the way a rooster pecks at his food—in little bits, the same way this salsa is chopped. Pico de Gallo is the perfect salsa for chip dipping. It's also darn good as a dip for fresh vegetables or as a spicy addition to everyday rice.

MAKES 2 CUPS

- 3 jalapeño chilies
- 3 large tomatoes
- 1 small white onion, peeled
- 2 cloves garlic, peeled
- $1/3$ cup fresh cilantro, chopped finely
- 1 tablespoon fresh lime juice
- 1 tablespoon fresh lemon juice
- 1 tablespoon red wine vinegar
- $1/2$ tablespoon olive oil
- $3/4$ teaspoon salt
- Freshly ground peppercorn to taste

For a milder salsa, start by removing and discarding the seeds and membranes from the jalapeños; then chop the chilies coarsely (about $1/8$- to $1/4$-inch cubes are good). Dice the tomatoes and onions to about the same size as the chilies. Mince the garlic finely. Place all the ingredients except the pepper in a bowl, toss to blend well, and let the salsa sit at room temperature for an hour. Mix in the pepper to taste and serve. Leftovers will keep in the refrigerator for 3 to 4 days, but Pico de Gallo tastes best on the day that you make it.

Maria's "No-Crackers-Allowed" Party Salsa

I used to work with Maria in this remote little California town called Tehachapi. This place is out in the middle of nowhere, up in the mountains above the Mojave Desert. Nothing ever happens in Tehachapi. I mean nothing. Okay, the wind blows, but that's about it. Anyway, in a place like that, almost any occasion qualifies as a party-worthy event: "Tomorrow's Friday? Let's have a party!"; "Your cat caught three tarantulas? I think we should have a party!"; "Hey, it looks like the winds are gusting above 60 miles an hour—we should have a party!" In our office, a party always meant that Maria would whip up some of her "No-Crackers-Allowed" Party Salsa. Bet you're wondering what "no-crackers-allowed" means, right? Well, Maria always mocked those who couldn't quite take her salsa's heat by calling them "crackers." Not exactly politically correct, but this is still a darn good salsa.

MAKES ABOUT 2 1/4 CUPS

- 1 to 6 jalapeño chilies*
- 1 can whole tomatoes, 16 ounces
- 1/2 cup fresh cilantro, chopped
- 1/2 small white onion, peeled

Start by roasting the chilies (see page 10 for directions). Allow them to cool to room temperature; then place them—seeds and all—in a blender with the tomatoes. Blend on medium speed for 10 seconds. Then add the cilantro and onion. Blend on medium speed for another 5 seconds. Refrigerate overnight and take it into your office the next day to celebrate the new company letterhead. Maria's salsa will keep in the refrigerator for up to 1 week, but I'll bet it won't last an hour after you bring it in to work.

*According to Maria, a 1- to 3-chili salsa is only fit for consumption by crackers. You have to include at least 4 chilies to start moving out of the cracker zone.

Uncle David's Alaskan Burly Man Salsa

My Uncle David is the quintessential Alaskan Burly Man. He's a fisherman, a hunter, an outdoorsman—and a maker of great salsa. You'll notice that the measurements for the ingredients are somewhat vague. That's because the true Alaskan Burly Man makes do with whatever he has on hand (which explains why there are airplanes in Alaska that are actually held together by duct tape.) Alaskan Burly Man Salsa goes best of all with tortilla chips, whisky in a dirty glass, and moose jerky—but feel free to enjoy it with anything that you'd normally eat with traditional tomato-based salsa.

MAKES AS MUCH AS THE INGREDIENTS YOU HAVE AVAILABLE WILL ALLOW

- 1 large can whole tomatoes (David refuses to specify a size—he just says "large," but 16 ounces is generally a good size.)
- Some fresh lemon juice (Two tablespoons is a good amount to start with.)
- 1 to 3 cloves garlic, peeled
- Some habañero chilies (Start with 1/2 chili, and work your way up to the desired hotness.)
- Other chilies to taste (Anaheim, jalapeño, and serrano are all good choices, but use whatever you can find.)
- 4 to 6 green onions
- Some (or none, depending on whether you like it and if it's available) fresh cilantro, chopped
- Enough salt

Drain the juice from the tomatoes and reserve it for some other purpose (such as bathing in after you've been sprayed by a skunk on a hunting expedition). Chop the drained tomatoes finely; if you're an Alaskan Burly Man, you'll use the lid from the tomato can for this purpose. Place the tomatoes in a bowl large enough to hold all the ingredients. Add the lemon juice. Chop the garlic and chilies finely. (If you want a cooler salsa, remove and discard the chili seeds first.) Mince the green onion. Add all the ingredients to the tomatoes and mix well. Serve immediately, or refrigerate for up to 4 days.

Cousin Irene's "Happy-Holidays-from-Colorado!" Salsa

I told my cousin Irene that if she really loved me, she'd send me her signature salsa more often than once a year during the holiday season. She responded by faxing me her recipe. I'm not sure exactly what she was trying to tell me. Anyway, because this salsa is canned, it's the perfect way to enjoy your abundant summer harvest of tomatoes year-round. Plus, it makes a great gift (hint, hint). It's wonderful with chips, omelets, or just about anything else!

MAKES ABOUT 5 TO 6 PINTS

- 10 cups tomatoes, peeled and seeded (See page 9 for tomato-peeling instructions.)
- 3 cups onions, peeled and chopped
- 1 1/4 cups chili peppers, seeded and chopped (Irene uses a combination of jalapeño, Anaheim, and serrano chilies.)
- 1 tablespoon fresh cilantro, chopped
- 1 cup commercial cider vinegar
- 6 cloves garlic, peeled and minced
- 1 tablespoon salt

Start by sterilizing six 1-pint jars. Wash and rinse the jars; then place them right-side up in a boiling-water bath canner and add hot water to cover them by at least 1 inch. Bring the water to a boil and boil the jars for 10 minutes. Turn the heat to low to keep the jars hot as you prepare the recipe. To prepare the canning jar lids, follow the manufacturer's instructions.

Chop the seeded tomatoes or blend them in a food processor. Then place them in a 6-quart saucepan and add the remaining ingredients. Bring the salsa to a boil, stirring occasionally. Reduce the heat and simmer about 30 minutes or until the salsa is the desired thickness.

Remove a canning jar from the canner and immediately fill it with salsa, leaving ½ inch of headspace (or space at the top of the jar). Remove any trapped air bubbles by running any non-metallic instrument (a chopstick or narrow spatula will work well) around the inside of the jar and up and down through the ingredients. Use a clean, damp cloth to wipe any drips from the rim and threaded portion of the jar. Then, using tongs or a canning lid "wand," lift a lid from the simmering water and place it on the jar. Tighten a screw band firmly down over the lid. Using jar lifters, place the jar back into the simmering water in the canner. Repeat to fill the other jars.

To process the salsa, start by placing the lid on the canner and turning the heat to high. Bring the water in the canner back to a full boil (this may take up to 30 minutes). Then set a timer and boil the jars for 15 minutes. If the water level in the canner begins to fall during processing, add simmering water to keep the jars covered by at least 1 inch.

Turn the heat off as soon as the jars have been processed for a full 15 minutes. Carefully remove the canner lid, tilting it away from you as you do to prevent steam burns. Using jar lifters, remove the jars and place them on a wooden board or folded towel to cool for 12 to 24 hours. Don't adjust the lids, even if they're loose.

When the jars are completely cool, remove the screw bands and check to make sure that the lids have sealed by pressing down on them with a finger or thumb; the lid shouldn't "give" at all. (The vacuum created as the salsa cools should draw each lid down into a concave position.) If the lid dips down when you press it—and stays down—the seal will probably be fine. If the lid springs back up when you press it, eat the salsa right away; the jar hasn't sealed properly!

Crunchy, Chewy, Sweet, and Spicy Salsa

(Or, if you must be prosaic—Jícama, Dried Apricot, Pineapple, and Chili Salsa)

You know how the raisins in your grandmother's Sunday-brunch carrot salad were always like a special little treat—a little extra sweet and chew in an otherwise (let's face it) bland dish? Well, the dried apricots in this recipe serve much the same function—except that this savory, sassy salsa hardly qualifies as bland! In fact, why not give Grandma (and yourself) a break this Sunday, and replace the traditional roast beef and carrot salad with grilled tuna (or any other fish) and Crunchy, Chewy, Sweet, and Spicy Salsa?

MAKES ABOUT 2¼ CUPS

- ¼ small, ripe pineapple
- ⅙ medium jícama (or about ¼ pound), peeled
- ¼ cup dried apricots
- ½ small red onion, peeled
- ¼ to ½ habañero chili
- ¼ cup fresh cilantro, chopped finely and packed
- Salt to taste

Peel and core the pineapple (see page 15 for pineapple-peeling advice). Dice 1 cup of pineapple into ¼-inch cubes; save the remaining fruit for another recipe. Dice the jícama into ¼-inch cubes. Chop the apricots and onion into ⅛- to ¼-inch pieces. Mince the chili finely—seeds, membranes, and all. (Of course, if just the idea of that much added heat makes you sweat, remove and discard the seeds and membranes before mincing.) Combine all the ingredients in a bowl and toss to mix well. Add salt to taste; then chill for 30 minutes before serving. This salsa should be consumed the same day it's made.

Day-After-Halloween Pumpkin Seed Salsa

November 1: You've consumed more sugar in the past 24 hours than you normally eat over a period of 6 months. You're asking yourself why you always buy 10 pounds of fun-size candy bars when you know you won't have more than three trick-or-treaters the whole night. It's the day after Halloween and your taste buds could use a serious jolt to knock them back to reality. You also need to do something with all those seeds you salvaged when you carved the jack-o'-lantern. This salsa is the perfect solution. Savory, spicy, and chock full of healthy vitamins, Pumpkin Seed Salsa is the perfect cure for the day-after-Halloween sugar crash. Try it with cheese enchiladas or as quesadilla filling, or use it as a garnish for any Mexican meal.

MAKES ABOUT 3 1/2 CUPS

- 1 cup corn kernels (fresh or frozen)
- 4 plum tomatoes
- 1 Anaheim chili, roasted (see page 10)
- 1 jalapeño chili, roasted (see page 10)
- 1 cup unsalted pumpkin seeds, toasted (See the directions on the following page for toasting pumpkin seeds.)
- 1 lime
- 1 teaspoon olive oil
- 1/3 teaspoon ground cumin
- 1/8 teaspoon freshly ground peppercorn
- Salt to taste

If you're using fresh corn, cut the kernels from the cobs using a very sharp knife. Heat a large frying pan over medium heat. Add the fresh or frozen corn kernels to the hot pan and roast for 5 to 7 minutes, stirring constantly. Remove the corn from the heat, place it in a bowl large enough to hold all the ingredients, and allow it to cool to room temperature. Chop the tomatoes coarsely and mince the whole chilies (or remove and discard the seeds and membranes for a less fiery salsa). Add the tomatoes, chilies, and pumpkin seeds to the corn. Juice the lime, remove any seeds, and pour the juice into a small bowl. Add the olive oil, cumin, and peppercorn to the lime juice and mix well. Pour the juice mixture over the corn and pumpkin seed mixture. Toss to blend, add salt to taste, and allow to sit at room temperature for 30 minutes before serving. Store any leftovers in the refrigerator for up to 2 days.

Toasting Pumpkin Seeds

Most health-food stores carry unsalted, toasted pumpkin seeds, but toasting your own is really easy and it gives you something to do with your jack-o-lantern's innards. Here's how you do it: Wash the seeds well with cool water and remove any pulp clinging to them. Preheat the oven to 375°F and spread the seeds in an even layer on a baking sheet. Bake for 20 to 30 minutes, or until the seeds are completely dry. Allow the seeds to cool to room temperature before using.

White Bean and Avocado Salsa for the Meek

Maybe you're looking for something that's not going to put hair on your chest, or possibly your tongue just needs a little cool down. Well, you've turned to the right page. This recipe is taste-able proof that salsa doesn't always have to be about flame (and pain). Here, for the tender-tongued among you, is a great-tasting, traditional-style salsa that's 100 percent burn-free. A nice nacho-topper, White Bean and Avocado Salsa for the Meek is also delicious with scrambled eggs.

MAKES ABOUT 2 CUPS

- 1/2 cup canned navy beans
- 1 Haas avocado
- 3 plum tomatoes
- 1/2 medium red onion, peeled
- 1 tablespoon sesame seeds
- 1 tablespoon fresh cilantro, chopped (optional)
- 1/2 lime
- 1 teaspoon olive oil
- Pinch of Mexican oregano
- Pinch of ground cumin (optional)
- Salt to taste

Rinse and drain the beans; then place them in a bowl large enough to hold all the ingredients. Peel the avocado and remove and discard its pit. Dice the avocado, tomatoes, and onion into cubes about the size of the beans; then add the diced ingredients, cilantro, and sesame seeds to the beans. Squeeze the juice from the lime, remove and discard any seeds, and pour the juice into a small bowl. Add the olive oil, oregano, and cumin to the lime juice and mix well. Pour the juice and oil mixture over the bean mixture. Toss well to blend and add salt to taste. Allow the salsa to sit at room temperature for 30 minutes before serving, or store in the refrigerator for up to 3 to 4 days.

Cilantro-Fanatic's Salsa

Yes, there are actually people out there who don't like cilantro. If you happen to be one of those crazed individuals, I suggest that you quickly turn to another page, because this recipe is for serious cilantro aficionados only. Hot, tart, and—well—cilantro-y, this salsa is great for chip-dipping. Cilantro lovers will almost certainly find at least 389 other uses for it, too.

MAKES ABOUT 1 3/4 CUPS

- 8 to 10 cloves garlic, peeled
- 1 tablespoon olive oil
- 2 jalapeño chilies
- 2 serrano chilies
- 2 cups fresh cilantro, chopped and packed tightly
- 2 limes
- Salt to taste

Preheat the oven to 300°F. Arrange the garlic cloves on a baking sheet and drizzle them with the olive oil. Bake for 1 hour, or until tender. Remove from the oven and allow to cool to room temperature. Mince the garlic finely. Remove and discard the seeds and membranes from the jalapeño and serrano chilies. Chop the chilies finely. Juice the limes, remove any seeds, and pour the juice into a blender with all the other ingredients except the salt. Process on high speed for about 10 seconds, or until the salsa is smooth, but not liquified. Add salt to taste. Allow the salsa to sit at room temperature for 30 minutes before serving. Cilantro-Fanatic's Salsa will keep in the refrigerator for 2 to 3 days.

Summer Harvest Peach, Apple, and Pear Salsa

Fresh peaches, tart apples, sweet pears—sounds like a walk through your local farmer's market, doesn't it? It also sounds like a recipe for a delicious and unusual salsa. If you're looking for an easy way to make an ordinary meal of roast pork or grilled chicken special, Summer Harvest Salsa is it.

MAKES ABOUT 2½ CUPS

- 2 large, firm, ripe peaches
- 1 Granny Smith apple
- 1 small, firm pear
- ½ cup fresh cilantro, chopped finely
- 2 tablespoons fresh mint, chopped finely (optional)
- ½ lime
- 3½ tablespoons honey
- ¼ teaspoon ground cinnamon
- ⅛ teaspoon ground nutmeg
- 2 cloves, ground
- Pinch of ground coriander (optional)

In a large saucepan over high heat, boil enough water to cover the peaches. Add the peaches to the boiling water and cook for 30 seconds; then transfer them to a bowl of cold water and soak for 1 minute. Drain and peel the peaches; then remove and discard their pits. Peel and core the apple and pear. Dice the peaches, apple, and pear into ¼-inch cubes and place them in a bowl large enough to hold all the ingredients. Add the cilantro and mint. Squeeze the juice from the lime, remove any seeds, and pour the juice into a small bowl. Add the honey, cinnamon, nutmeg, ground cloves, and coriander to the lime juice. Stir to mix well; then pour over the peach, apple, and pear mixture. Chill for 30 minutes before serving. This salsa should be used on the same day it's made.

Genevieve's Berry Good Hunter-Gatherer Salsa

My mom Genevieve has the heart and soul of a prehistoric-era hunter-gatherer. Her penchant for hand-picking wild berries is probably the best example. This unusual salsa is another great way in which she uses the fruits of her hunting-gathering labors. Try baking my mom's salsa on salmon or any other fish. Or, omit the green onion, garlic, chili, and vinegar, and add another tablespoon of honey to make a tasty topping for ice cream.

MAKES ABOUT 1¼ CUPS

- 2 green onions
- 1 clove garlic, peeled
- 1 jalapeño chili
- ½ cup blackberries
- ⅓ cup raspberries
- ⅓ cup whole (not jellied) cranberry sauce
- 2 tablespoons blackberry liqueur
- 1½ tablespoons honey
- 1 teaspoon raspberry vinegar.

Mince the green onions and garlic finely. Remove and discard the seeds and membranes from the chili; then dice the chili finely. If the blackberries are large (longer than ¾ inch), cut them in half. Place the onions, garlic, chili, berries, and cranberry sauce in a bowl large enough to hold all the ingredients. Combine the liqueur, honey, and vinegar in a separate bowl. Blend well; then pour over the berry mixture. Mix gently to coat all the ingredients. Use immediately or keep in the refrigerator for up to 2 days.

"Get-Your-Protein" Black Bean and Roasted Corn Salsa

Vegetarians (and cows everywhere) rejoice! Served with rice, this good-looking salsa forms a complete, balanced protein. As an added bonus, it tastes great, too. Black Bean and Roasted Corn Salsa is mighty fine with tortilla chips, but my favorite way to enjoy it is in a quesadilla, with loads of melted Monterey jack cheese. If you've never made a quesadilla before, check out the very easy recipe and instructions on the following page.

MAKES ABOUT 2 1/4 CUPS

- 1 cup frozen corn or 2 to 3 ears fresh corn
- 1/2 cup black beans, canned or cooked
- 1/2 small green bell pepper
- 1/2 small red bell pepper
- 2 serrano chilies
- 1/4 small red onion, peeled
- 2 cloves garlic, peeled
- 3 green onions
- 1/3 cup fresh cilantro, chopped
- 1/4 cup olive oil
- 1 lime
- 1 teaspoon dried Mexican oregano
- Salt to taste

If you're using fresh corn, cut the kernels from the cobs using a very sharp knife. (Discard the corn cobs.) Heat a large frying pan over medium heat. Add the fresh or frozen corn kernels to the hot pan and roast for 5 to 7 minutes, stirring constantly. Remove the corn from the heat, place it in a bowl large enough to hold all the ingredients, and allow it to cool to room temperature. Drain and discard all the canning or cooking liquid from the black beans. Add the beans to the corn. Remove and discard the seeds from the bell peppers and chilies; then chop the peppers into 1/8- to 1/4-inch cubes. Mince the chilies and garlic finely. Dice the red and green onions to the same size as the peppers. Add the peppers, chilies, onions, garlic, and cilantro to the corn and beans. Juice the lime, remove any seeds, and pour the juice into a small bowl. Add the olive oil and Mexican oregano. Stir well; then pour over the corn and bean mixture.

Mix well and add salt to taste. Allow the salsa to sit at room temperature for an hour before serving. This salsa will keep in the refrigerator for 3 to 4 days.

Making Quesadillas

Salsas make perfect fillings for quesadillas. If you've never made these tasty, recently-chic "sandwiches," you're about to find out what an easy business it is—although not quite as easy my former roommate's boyfriend liked to make it. He'd fold a flour tortilla around a couple of slices of American cheese and stick the resulting sandwich in the microwave for 30 seconds. Then he'd top the thing off with—eeeek!—store-bought salsa. I call that "Guy Cuisine." I hope that the simple directions that follow will help men everywhere—and, yes, women, too!—overcome the urge to make "Guy Cuisine" quesadillas.

FOR EACH QUESADILLA:

Cooking spray

2 flour tortillas, 6 to 9 inches in diameter

2 to 3 ounces cheese, grated (Monterey jack or cheddar)

2 to 3 tablespoons salsa of your choice

Sour cream and additional salsa for garnish

Lightly coat a medium frying pan with cooking spray; then warm the pan over medium heat. You'll assemble the quesadilla while the pan is getting hot. Your best bet is to do this close to the stove top—you're going to have to transfer the completed sandwich to the hot frying pan, and the less distance you have to cover, the better. That said, lay one tortilla flat on a cutting board or plate. Sprinkle half the cheese on top of the tortilla in an even layer. Spread the salsa evenly over the cheese; then sprinkle the remaining cheese on top of the salsa. Press the other tortilla into place on top of the cheese. Carefully place the quesadilla in the hot pan. Cook for about 5 minutes, or until the cheese on the bottom side has melted completely and the bottom tortilla is golden brown. Coat the top tortilla with a light mist of cooking spray; then turn the quesadilla and cook for about 5 more minutes. Remove from the pan, cut into quarters or eighths, and serve with sour cream, additional salsa, and rice. Now, wasn't that easy?

Roasted Habañero Salsa

Like it hot? Like it real *hot? Lucky you—this salsa's a scorcher! But it's not all about heat, mind you. The habañero has a well-earned reputation as one of tastiest as well as one the hottest chilies around. If you're really brave, you might try dipping a chip or two in this one (although the chip might disintegrate before it reaches your mouth—a subtle warning you may or may not choose to heed). For the not-as-brave (or should I say, "not-as-foolish"?), a hearty grilled steak makes a very suitable companion for this sizzling salsa.*

MAKES ABOUT 1 CUP

- 3 habañero chilies
- 3 plum tomatoes
- ¼ cup water
- ⅛ teaspoon salt
- ⅛ teaspoon ground cumin

Warm a medium frying pan over medium-low heat. Place the chilies and tomatoes in the hot pan and roast for 25 to 30 minutes, turning occasionally to brown evenly on all sides. Remove the tomatoes and chilies from the heat and allow them to cool to room temperature. Remove and discard the seeds from the chilies. Place all the ingredients in a blender and process on medium-high speed until smooth. Allow the salsa to sit at room temperature for 1 hour before serving. Keep Roasted Habañero Salsa in the refrigerator for up to 24 hours, but let it return to room temperature again before serving.

Heavenly Avocado Salsa

Creamy avocadoes, tart lime juice, pungent onion—you can almost taste why I call this salsa "heavenly" just by reading the ingredients, can't you? I like Heavenly Avocado Salsa unadulterated, served with nothing but warm tortilla chips, but it's also great with grilled steaks or on top of cheddar-cheese cheeseburgers. Let the angels sing!

MAKES ABOUT 2 CUPS

- 2 large Haas avocadoes
- 1 lime
- 1 small white onion, peeled
  (For the best flavor, use a sweet variety such as Vidalia or Bermuda.)
- 3 plum tomatoes
- 1 clove garlic, peeled
- 1/4 to 1 habañero chili
- 1/2 yellow bell pepper
- Salt to taste
- Freshly ground peppercorn to taste

Peel the avocadoes and remove and discard their seeds. Place the avocadoes in a bowl large enough to hold all the ingredients. Juice the lime, remove any seeds, and add the juice to the avocadoes. Use a fork to mash the avocadoes and lime juice to a chunky paste. Refrigerate while you prepare the other ingredients. Chop the onion and tomatoes into 1/8-inch cubes. Mince the garlic finely. Remove and discard the seeds and membranes from the chili and pepper. Mince the chili finely and chop the pepper into 1/8-inch cubes. Add all the ingredients to the avocado paste and mix well. Serve immediately—this salsa won't last long.

Pineapple-Mango "Tropical-Paradise-in-a-Bowl" Salsa

Combine one part Caribbean sunshine with two parts island relaxation. Add a heaping dose of Calypso-style steel drums and three strands of sea-harvested moonbeams. Blend well by dancing the Merengue barefoot on a scorching-hot beach. Okay, so you might have a tough time finding those particular ingredients at your local grocery store, and maybe you don't know the Merengue (but that's what dance lessons are for, right?). Fortunately, you can make a few easy-to-find substitutions (indicated in the recipe below) and end up with a salsa that tastes remarkably like the one described above. Turn a fish taco into a fiesta by topping it with a heaping spoonful of this bright and flavorful concoction. Pineapple-Mango Salsa also goes well with grilled fish, vegetables, or chicken.

MAKES ABOUT 3½ CUPS

- 1 fresh, ripe pineapple
- 1 ripe mango
- ½ cup red cabbage
- ½ small red onion, peeled
- ¼ cup fresh cilantro, chopped
- 2 tablespoons fresh lime juice
- ½ to 1 habañero chili
- Pinch of ground coriander

Peel and core the pineapple (see page 15). Dice 1½ cups of the pineapple into ¼-inch cubes. Reserve the rest for another purpose (homemade piña coladas, for instance, and—how 'bout that?—there just happens to be a recipe for them on the next page). Peel the mango and remove and discard its seed. Dice the mango, cabbage, and onion into ⅛-inch cubes. Remove and discard the seeds from the chili; then mince the chili finely. Combine all the ingredients in a bowl and mix well. Refrigerate for 1 hour before serving. This salsa will keep for up to 2 days in the refrigerator.

Using that Spare Pineapple: Making Piña Coladas

Unless you're planning to feed the masses, you'll probably have some pineapple to spare after whipping up a batch of Pineapple-Mango "Paradise-in-a-Bowl" Salsa. And depending on how much habañero chili you used, you may find yourself groping for something—anything—to cool your scorched tongue. Well, here, on one convenient page, is the solution to both problems—the ever-popular piña colada. Smart chilehead that you are, you're saying to yourself, "No mere rum drink could possibly tame a habañero's flame!" And right you are. But this is no mere rum drink. This drink was specially designed for maximum capsicum relief. The secret? A generous helping of vanilla ice cream.

MAKES 6 SERVINGS

2 cups fresh pineapple, peeled, cored, and diced

1/2 cup pineapple juice

1/2 cup milk

1 1/2 cups unsweetened coconut cream (a canned, concentrated form of coconut milk available wherever liquor is sold)

1 1/2 cups light rum

1 cup vanilla ice cream

Pineapple chunks for garnish

Start by freezing the pineapple overnight. Place the pineapple, pineapple juice, and milk in the blender and blend until thoroughly liquified. Then add the coconut cream, rum, and ice cream. Blend well. Pour into glasses, garnish with pineapple chunks, and help yourself to another chip-full of habañero-heavy salsa.

Serious Chilehead Arbol-Cayenne Salsa

Yeah, that's right, all you chileheads. This recipe calls for—count 'em—10 to 14 chilies. And chiles de arbols and cayennes aren't exactly wimpy capsicums, either. I don't recommend attempting this one with tortilla chips. Try it with a sturdy beef burrito or taco instead—you'll be glad you did.

MAKES ABOUT 2½ CUPS

- 5 to 7 dried chiles de arbol or an equal number of dried cayenne chilies
- 5 to 7 dried cayenne chilies
- 8 tomatillos, husks removed
- 2 cloves garlic, peeled
- ¼ small yellow onion, peeled
- 2 to 3 tablespoons warm water
- ⅛ teaspoon cumin
- Salt to taste

Remove and save the seeds from the chilies. Warm a medium frying pan over medium heat and open a couple of windows to promote good ventilation (you'll need it for the next step). Place the chilies in the pan and toast for 7 to 10 minutes, turning occasionally to prevent burning. Remove the chilies and set them aside. Place the tomatillos and garlic in the pan. Toast and turn for 10 to 15 minutes, or until the tomatillos turn light green. Remove the tomatillos and garlic and set them aside; then reduce the heat to low and add the chili seeds to the pan. Toast for 5 minutes, or until the seeds turn golden brown, shaking the pan constantly. Turn off the heat and place the seeds in a blender with about ½ tablespoon of warm water. On high speed, pulse the blender to grind the seeds and water to a paste. Add the chilies one at a time, pulsing between each addition. Add more water as needed. Chop the tomatillos, garlic, and onion coarsely; then slowly add them to the chili paste, pulsing between each addition. Add the cumin and pulse once more. Scrap the paste into a bowl and, using a mortar or the back of a spoon, mash the paste thoroughly, making sure to crush any lumps. Allow the salsa to sit at room temperature for 30 minutes before serving, or store in the refrigerator for up to 3 days.

Salsa Verde

Green sauce—that's what the name means, and that's how the salsa looks. Ladle this wonderful, savory stuff on top of chicken enchiladas, spoon it over grilled fish, or serve it with a big basket of tortilla chips. Just make sure you have plenty on hand—Salsa Verde is mighty versatile and mighty addictive.

MAKES ABOUT 2 $1/2$ CUPS

- 1 large green tomato or substitute 4 tomatillos, husks removed
- 6 tomatillos, husks removed
- 1 serrano chili
- 1 clove garlic, peeled
- 1 small yellow onion, peeled
- $1/4$ cup fresh cilantro
- 1 tablespoon fresh lime juice
- $1/8$ teaspoon freshly ground peppercorn
- Salt to taste

Place the green tomato and the tomatillos in a saucepan. Cover them with water and simmer until tender. Drain and set them aside. Remove and discard the seeds and membranes from the chili, and coarsely chop the chili, garlic, and onion. When the tomato and tomatillos have cooled, place all the ingredients in a blender. Process on low or medium speed until the salsa is smooth, but not liquefied. Serve immediately or store in the refrigerator for 3 to 4 days.

Torrid Thai Salsa

The folks in Thailand know how to do hot right, as any Thai-food fan can tell you. Adjust your taste buds a few degrees to the East, turn in your tortillas for some fried wontons, and sample this spicy salsa from the Orient. But before you decide to whip this one up for an impromptu dinner party, note that you'll need to prepare one of the ingredients, the chili oil, a couple of weeks in advance. Alternatively, you may be able to find a bottle of commercial chili oil at your local Asian market.

Chili Oil
Makes 1 cup

- 1 cup sesame oil
- 8 whole peppercorns
- 2 to 5 dried Thai chilies

Sterilize a glass jar according to the instructions on page 29. Place the chilies and peppercorns in the jar and pour the oil over them. Seal the jar and store somewhere dark for 1 to 2 weeks before using.

Salsa
Makes about 1¾ cups

- 3 pickling cucumbers
- ⅓ cup radishes
- ½ bunch green onions
- 4 cloves garlic, peeled
- ¼ cup fresh mint, chopped
- 1½ tablespoons fresh lime juice
- 1¼ teaspoons chili oil
- 3 tablespoons fresh ginger, grated
- 1 tablespoon sugar
- 1 tablespoon sesame seeds
- Salt to taste

Peel the cucumbers, slice them in half lengthwise, and scoop out and discard the seeds. Dice the cucumbers and radishes into ⅛-inch cubes. Mince the green onions and garlic. Place the cucumbers, radishes, green onions, garlic, and mint in a bowl large enough to hold all the ingredients.

Combine the lime juice and chili oil in a small bowl. Add the ginger, sugar, and sesame seeds, and blend well. Pour the mixture over the other ingredients, toss gently to mix, and refrigerate for 1 hour before serving chilled. Torrid Thai Salsa will keep in the refrigerator for about 1 day.

Kay's Splendid Summer Salsa

During the summer months, my friend Kay grows a veritable supermarket's worth of produce in lovely pots on her back porch. To take advantage of this bounty, she created a mouth-watering summertime salsa that's a perfect mate for grilled chicken or fish.

MAKES ABOUT 1½ CUPS

- 1 fresh jalapeño chili
- ½ medium red bell pepper
- ½ large red onion, peeled
- 1 medium mango, peeled and seed removed
- ¼ cup fresh cilantro, chopped finely
- ¼ cup fresh mint, chopped finely
- 1 lime

Start by removing and discarding the seeds and membranes from the jalapeño chili and red bell pepper; then dice the chili and pepper finely and place them in a bowl large enough to hold all the ingredients. Chop the onion and mango to about the same size as the chili and the bell pepper and add them to the bowl. Toss in the cilantro and mint. Juice the lime, remove any seeds, and add the juice to the other ingredients. Blend well and allow to rest at room temperature for 1 hour before serving. Leftovers will keep in the refrigerator for up to 3 days, but this salsa tastes best served at room temperature on the same day you make it.

Peaches and Ginger Salsa

It's like a bodice-ripping romance novel! The sweet Southern belle from Georgia (let's call her "Peaches") meets a dashing and mysterious prince from India (we'll call him "Ginger"). The two come together in a passionate wedding of exotic flavors and textures. Oh, this salsa's a steamy one, alright. Tasty, too. You won't believe what it can do for grilled lamb chops, Cornish game hens, or (heaving) chicken breasts.

MAKES ABOUT 3 CUPS

- 6 to 8 ripe peaches
- 1 small red bell pepper
- 1 small green bell pepper
- 1/2 serrano chili
- 1/2 jalapeño chili
- 1 small red onion, peeled
- 1/4 cup fresh mint, chopped
- 1 tablespoon fresh lime juice
- 3 teaspoons fresh ginger, grated
- 2 teaspoons olive oil
- Salt to taste

Peel and pit the peaches. Dice them into ¼-inch cubes and place them in a bowl large enough to hold all the ingredients. Remove and discard the seeds and membranes from the bell peppers and chilies. Dice the bell peppers and onion to the same size as the peaches, and mince the chilies finely. Add the peppers, onion, chilies, and mint to the peaches. Toss gently to mix. In a small bowl, combine the lime juice, ginger, and olive oil. Blend well; then pour over the peach mixture. Add salt to taste, mix gently, and refrigerate for at least 30 minutes before serving. Peaches and Ginger Salsa will keep in the refrigerator for 1 to 2 days.

Spicy-Sweet Melon Salsa

For those of you who don't live in a big city with a lot of trendy restaurants, this salsa's probably going to sound a little weird to you. And sure, it is a little weird. But keep in mind that some weird things are much more intriguing than their run-of-the-mill counterparts—just think of that guy in your junior-high biology class. So he wore geeky clothes and always seemed to smell like formaldehyde—did anyone else in your class go on to win a Nobel Peace Prize? I think not. My point is: Give this salsa a try. It's outstanding teamed with grilled turkey or chicken breasts and, although you probably won't win a Nobel Peace Prize with it, you will impress the heck out of your friends with your originality, daring, and good taste.

MAKES 2 CUPS

1 jalapeño chili

1 cup watermelon, rind and seeds removed

1 cup honeydew melon, rind and seeds removed

4 tablespoons fresh chives, chopped finely

1 tablespoon fresh cilantro, chopped finely

½ teaspoon sugar

Salt to taste

Start by removing and discarding the seeds and membranes from the chili. Then mince the chili finely and place it in a bowl large enough to hold all the ingredients. Chop the watermelon and honeydew into ¼-inch cubes and add them to the chili with all the other ingredients except the salt. Toss gently to mix well and add salt to taste. This salsa won't keep—the watermelon's too juicy—so serve it within an hour of making it.

Cindy's "Oh Hell, I Don't Have A Date Anyway, So Why Not?" Garlic Salsa

I used to call this one Cindy's "Kiss-Me-Not" Garlic Salsa, but since I'm not exactly being bombarded with kisses these days, I decided not to turn any down before they're offered. Actually, this is such a good salsa that I'd probably choose it over most kisses, anyway. If you are feeling a little amorous, just be sure that both you and the object of your affection have a few chip-fulls of this garlicky delight before moving on to other activities. Simply entice your amoré with a heaping plate of cheddar cheese and Garlic Salsa nachos—love at first bite!

MAKES ABOUT 2 CUPS

- 10 to 12 cloves garlic, peeled
- ¼ cup plus 1 tablespoon olive oil
- 3 medium tomatoes
- 1 pickling cucumber
- 1 small red onion, peeled
- 2 serrano chilies
- 1 lemon
- 4 tablespoons fresh chives, chopped finely
- 2 tablespoons fresh cilantro, chopped finely
- Salt to taste
- Freshly ground peppercorn to taste

Preheat the oven to 300°F. Place the garlic cloves on a baking sheet and drizzle 1 tablespoon of olive oil over them. Bake for 1 hour, or until the garlic has softened. Allow the cloves to cool; then mince finely and set aside. Peel the tomatoes (see page 9 for instructions), cut them into quarters, and remove and discard the seeds. Chop the tomatoes coarsely (¼-inch cubes are a good size). Peel the cucumber, slice it in half lengthwise, and scoop out and discard the seeds. Chop the cucumber and onion to the same size as the tomatoes. Remove and discard the seeds and membranes from the chilies; then mince the chilies finely. Place the garlic, tomatoes, cucumber, onion, and chilies in a bowl large enough to hold all the ingredients. Juice the lemon, remove any seeds, and pour the juice into a separate bowl. Add the remaining olive oil to the lemon juice, along with the chives and cilantro. Blend the ingredients well; then pour over the vegetable mixture. Toss to mix and add salt and pepper to taste. Chill in the refrigerator for 1 hour before serving. This salsa will keep in the refrigerator for 2 to 3 days.

Shelby's Boise-Style Cranberry Salsa

Yes, Boise. After all, Idaho's not just about potatoes anymore. Now it's about darn good cranberry salsa, too. This one is great with chips and even better with chicken or turkey. Heck, why not spice up your bland, traditional Thanksgiving dinner with this spicy treat from Idaho? Just be sure to warn Grandma first—a couple of jalapeño chilies give Shelby's Boise-Style Cranberry Salsa a little kick she might not be expecting.

MAKES ABOUT 2 CUPS

- 6 green onions
- 2 to 3 jalapeño chilies
- 2 sixteen-ounce cans whole (not jellied) cranberry sauce
- 1 cup fresh cilantro, chopped finely
- 1 teaspoon ground cumin

Chop the green onions very finely. Remove and discard the seeds and membranes from the jalapeños; then chop the chilies very finely. Place all the ingredients in a bowl, mix well, and refrigerate for 12 hours before serving. This salsa will keep in the refrigerator for up to 1 week.

Cindy's Life-Changing Pineapple and Chipotle Salsa

If you're wondering why I call this salsa "life-changing," take a minute to turn back to page 6 and read the introduction. Although Pineapple and Chipotle Salsa makes a tasty and unusual dip for tortilla chips, its real soul mate is Jamaican Jerk Chicken. And just because I'm feeling generous, I've included a recipe for said soul mate on the next page.

MAKES ABOUT 3½ CUPS

- 1 large fresh ripe pineapple
- 1 green bell pepper
- 1 red bell pepper
- 1 large red onion, peeled
- 1 green onion
- 2 to 5 chipotle chilies
- ¼ cup cilantro, chopped
- 2 limes
- ¼ cup sugar or to taste
- 1 teaspoon sesame seeds
- ⅛ teaspoon garlic powder
- 1 teaspoon ground coriander
- 1½ teaspoons ground cumin
- Dash of cinnamon
- Dash of allspice
- 1 teaspoon salt or to taste

Peel and core the pineapple, discarding the skin and core (see page 15 for pineapple-peeling tips); then chop the pineapple into ¼-inch cubes. Remove and discard the seeds and membranes from the bell peppers; then dice the peppers and onions into ¼-inch pieces. Mince the chilies finely. Place the pineapple, peppers, onion, chilies, and cilantro in a bowl large enough to hold all the ingredients. Grate the peel from the limes and set the peel aside. Cut the limes in half and juice them, removing and discarding the seeds. In a small bowl, combine the grated lime peel, lime juice, and the remaining ingredients. Blend well; then pour over the pineapple mixture. Refrigerate for at least 1 hour before serving. This salsa will keep for 2 to 3 days in the refrigerator.

Jamaican Jerk Chicken

Their eyes met across the table. Electricity seemed to fill the air. When they finally touched, everyone present knew it was a match made in heaven. I'm talking about the special relationship between Jamaican Jerk Chicken and Pineapple Chipotle Salsa, of course. If ever two foods were meant to be together, these are the two. As promised, here's a recipe for Jamaican Jerk Chicken. Actually, I'll start with a recipe for Jamaican Jerk Marinade; then we'll get down to business with the chicken.

JAMAICAN JERK MARINADE
MAKES ABOUT 2 CUPS

- 1 to 10 habañero chilies, seeds removed and chopped
- 1 onion, peeled and chopped
- 3 green onions, chopped
- 3 cloves garlic, peeled and chopped
- 1 tablespoon ground coriander
- 2 tablespoons salt
- 1/2 tablespoon fresh ginger, grated
- 2 teaspoons freshly ground peppercorn
- 1/2 teaspoon ground cumin
- 1/2 teaspoon paprika
- 2 teaspoons dried thyme
- 2 teaspoons ground allspice
- 1 teaspoon ground cinnamon
- 1/2 teaspoon ground cloves
- 1/2 teaspoon ground nutmeg
- 1/4 cup white vinegar
- 3 tablespoons olive oil
- 1 tablespoon brown sugar
- 3 tablespoons water

Grind all the ingredients to a paste in a blender. Although this marinade will keep indefinitely in the refrigerator, it's at its most flavorful during the first week.

Jamaican Jerk Chicken

    2 pounds chicken pieces, washed and patted dry
    1 1/2 cups Jamaican Jerk Marinade
    Melted butter for basting
    Lime wedges for garnish

Rub the marinade all over the chicken and under its skin. Let the meat marinate in the refrigerator for 24 hours. Light the grill and let the charcoal burn until it turns ashy and white all over. Push all the charcoal to one side of the grill and adjust the heat to low. Place the chicken on the side of the grill opposite the charcoal. Cover the grill and cook for 30 to 40 minutes, basting with melted butter every 10 to 15 minutes. The chicken is done when the meat pulls away easily from the bones and the juices run clear. Garnish with wedges of fresh lime and serve with—what else?—Pineapple Chipotle Salsa.

Kay's Fit-for-the-Gods (and Goddesses) Greek Salsa

Maybe you don't think "Greek" when you think "salsa." If that's the case, you need to think again. This Mediterranean-inspired recipe is perfect for folks who love intense salsa flavor, but who aren't so hot about intense salsa heat. Add a few spoonfuls to an ordinary dinner salad, bake it over chicken breasts, or serve it all on its own as a sassy side dish. But before you get started, keep Kay's caution in mind: Don't even think you can make this salsa unless you've got vine-picked tomatoes so ripe that their juices drip through your fingers as you slice them.

MAKES ABOUT 2 3/4 CUPS

- 3 medium tomatoes
- 2 pickling cucumbers
- 1 red onion, peeled
- 1/4 cup Greek olives
- 1/4 cup feta cheese
- 1/4 teaspoon fresh oregano
- 1 lemon

Dice the tomatoes into ¼-inch cubes. Peel the cucumbers, slice them in half lengthwise, and scoop out and discard their seeds. Dice the cucumbers into ¼-inch cubes. Slice the onion very thinly (less than 1/16 inch thick). Cut the olives into halves (or quarters, if they're very large). Place the tomatoes, cucumbers, onion, and olives in a bowl large enough to hold all the ingredients. Crumble the feta cheese into the bowl and add the oregano. Juice the lemon, remove any seeds, and add the juice to the other ingredients. Toss to blend well and chill for at least 4 hours before serving. This salsa will keep in the refrigerator for about 4 days.

Brian's "Homesick-for-Miami" Mango and Habañero Salsa

When my friend Brian (who asked that I refer to him here as "a gorgeous hunk of a man") first moved to western North Carolina from Miami, he was always whining about the southern Appalachian region's lack of spicy cuisine. So I said to him one day, "If you don't like our food, why don't you make your own? No one's stopping you, you know." A few weeks later, Brian dropped by with a sample of his newly-concocted, Miami-inspired salsa. Blessed day! What a magnificent creation. Try it with sweet-potato chips, grilled vegetables, grilled fish, pork, or chicken. Be careful with those habañero chilies, though—they're dangerously hot. Brian ended up scorching his tongue on an overly-fiery batch of salsa, and is now restricted to a diet of fried pork rinds and ketchup.

MAKES ABOUT 2½ CUPS

- 3 large, ripe mangoes
- 1 pickling cucumber
- ¼ to 1 habañero chili
- ¼ cup fresh mint, chopped finely
- 1 lime
- 2 teaspoons fresh ginger, grated
- 1 tablespoon tightly packed brown sugar
- Salt to taste
- Freshly ground peppercorn to taste

Peel the mangoes, remove and discard their pits, and dice the mango flesh coarsely (¼-inch cubes are a good size). Peel the cucumber, slice it in half lengthwise, and scoop out and discard the seeds. Dice the cucumber to the same size as the mango flesh. Remove and discard the seeds from the habañero; then mince the chili finely. Place the mangoes, cucumber, chili, and mint in a bowl large enough to hold all the ingredients. Juice the lime, remove any seeds, and pour the juice into a small bowl. Add the ginger and sugar and stir well. Pour the juice mixture over the mango mixture and blend well. Add salt and pepper to taste. Refrigerate for 1 hour before serving. This salsa will keep for 2 to 3 days in the refrigerator.

Beach-Blanket-Baby Horseradish Salsa

Just why do you think Annette Funicello always looked so darn perky in all those 1960s teen-queen beach flicks? If you guessed Frankie Avalon, you're wrong. I have proof (okay, I have an eighth-hand, completely unfounded, probably totally false rumor) that Annette loved shellfish, and she got plenty of them while filming those movies. Well, if she'd had access to this made-for-shellfish salsa, I bet she would have shattered the old perk-o-meter with her new-found enthusiasm. Spoon a dab of this piquant salsa on steamed clams, oysters on the half shell, or smoked mussels. I guarantee it will make you the star of your next neighborhood clambake.

MAKES ABOUT 3/4 CUP

- 1 large tomato
- 2 green onions
- 2 tablespoons fresh cilantro, chopped finely and packed tightly
- 1 tablespoon prepared horseradish
- 1/4 tablespoon salt or to taste
- 1/2 teaspoon freshly ground peppercorn or to taste
- Pinch of ground coriander

Peel the tomato (see page 9 for instructions), cut it into quarters, and gently remove and discard the seeds. Chop the tomato finely and place it in a bowl large enough to hold all the ingredients. Mince the green onions and add them and all the remaining ingredients to the tomato. Toss gently to mix well. Refrigerate for at least 1 hour before serving. This salsa doesn't keep well, so plan to make and eat it on the same day.

Grandma Nannie's Cucumber Salsa

I don't have a Grandma Nannie, but my friend Kay most certainly does—lucky for all of us! Pair Grandma's cool cucumber salsa with grilled fish, or do as Kay does and eat it all by itself, straight from the bowl.

MAKES 3 TO 4 CUPS

- 5 to 8 pickling cucumbers
- 1 1/2 tablespoons salt
- 3 tablespoons rice wine vinegar
- 1 tablespoon dried dill or 1/2 tablespoon fresh dill, chopped finely
- 1/2 onion, peeled (A sweet variety such as Vidalia or Bermuda tastes best in this recipe.)
- 1 teaspoon freshly ground peppercorn
- 3 tablespoons reduced-fat sour cream

Peel the cucumbers and cut them into very thin slices (about 1/16 inch is a good thickness). Place the cucumbers in a colander, add the salt, and toss well by hand. Allow to rest for 30 minutes. Rinse well under cool, running water; then gently squeeze out as much moisture as possible with your hands. Set aside.

Blend the vinegar and dill in a bowl large enough to hold all the ingredients. Then slice the onion to the same thickness as the cucumbers and add it to the bowl. Add the pepper. Then add the cucumbers and sour cream, mix gently to blend well, and chill for at least 4 hours. This salsa will keep for up to 3 days in the refrigerator, but Kay says you'll probably eat it all long before then!

Yummy California-Style Gingered Dessert Salsa

When I moved to California from North Carolina several years ago, my mother would call me up about once a week to ask if I'd seen any movie stars or turned into a surfer chick yet. I've been trying to convince her ever since that there's a lot more going on in the Golden State than Hollywood and beaches—innovative cuisine, for instance. Gingered Dessert Salsa is a great example. Served over vanilla ice cream or frozen yogurt, this salsa makes a delicious, unusual, and very Californian dessert.

MAKES ABOUT 1½ CUPS

- ½ cup raspberries
- 2 tablespoons sugar
- 1 small, ripe mango
- ¼ fresh pineapple
- ½ cup fresh strawberries, decapped
- 3½ tablespoons crystallized ginger, minced finely
- ½ teaspoon balsamic vinegar

In a bowl large enough to hold all the ingredients, coarsely crush together the raspberries and sugar. Remove and discard the peel and pit from the mango. Peel and core the pineapple (see page 15 for pineapple-peeling tips). Dice the mango, strawberries, and ½ cup of pineapple (save the remaining pineapple for another use) into ⅛-inch cubes. Add all the ingredients to the raspberries and sugar, and mix well. Serve immediately—this salsa doesn't keep well.

Desert Delight Cactus Salsa

You've heard about the population explosions Phoenix and Las Vegas have been experiencing over the last few years, right? And sure, who wouldn't want to move some place where the mercury regularly reaches 110°F? Well, if you've puzzled over this demographic trend, puzzle no more. The reason folks are moving to the desert Southwest in droves is the cactus. Yes, the cactus. It's delicious—especially in salsa. But thanks to ever-more widely-available canned cactus, you may now enjoy this desert delight without ever leaving your hometown. Tuck a spoonful of this unusual treat in a beef or chicken taco, or eat it plain with chips. All the pleasures of desert living and none of the heat stroke. What could be nicer?

MAKES ABOUT 2 CUPS

- 1⅓ cups canned or bottled prickly-pear cactus paddles*
- ⅙ medium jicama (or about ¼ pound), peeled
- 2 plum tomatoes
- ½ small yellow onion, peeled
- 1 serrano chili
- 1 clove garlic, peeled
- ¼ cup fresh cilantro, chopped
- 1 lime
- 1 tablespoon olive oil
- Pinch of cumin
- Salt to taste
- Freshly ground peppercorn to taste

Place the cactus in a colander or sieve and rinse it under cold, running water. Drain the cactus well; then chop it into ½-inch cubes. Chop the jicama, tomatoes, and onion into ¼-inch pieces. Remove and discard the seeds from the chili; then dice the chili and garlic finely. Place the cactus, jicama, tomatoes, onion, chili, garlic, and cilantro in a bowl large enough to hold all the ingredients. Squeeze the juice from the lime, remove and discard any seeds, and place the juice in a small bowl. Add the olive oil and cumin to the lime juice, mix well, and pour over the cactus mixture. Stir gently to blend, add salt and pepper to taste, and refrigerate for 1 hour before serving. Desert Delight Cactus Salsa will keep in the refrigerator for about 1 day.

*Commercially available prickly pear cactus is often called "nopalito." It can be found in most Latin American markets and many well-stocked grocery stores.

Acknowledgments

Thank you, thank you, thank you *to the following wonderful people who contributed recipes, know-how, and/or humor, inspiration, and support to the production of this book:*

STEVE ATKINS
(Bellevue, Washington)

GENEVIEVE AND LARRY BURDA
(Mars Hill, North Carolina)

KAY AND JOE BUTLER
(Mars Hill, North Carolina)

BRIAN CASKEY
(Asheville, North Carolina)

IRENE HEIL
(Longmont, Colorado)

LARAMÉE LYDA AND JEFF CRAFT
(Bakersfield, California)

CHRIS RICH
(Asheville, North Carolina)

MARIA SANCHEZ
(Tehachapi, California)

SHELBY WEAVER
(Boise, Idaho)

DAVID WHITMIRE
(Homer, Alaska)

Index to Recipes

Beach-Blanket-Baby Horseradish Salsa, 57

Brian's "Homesick-for-Miami" Mango and Habañero Salsa, 56

Cilantro Fanatic's Salsa, 35

Cindy's Life-Changing Pineapple and Chipotle Salsa, 52

Cindy's "Oh Hell, I Don't Have a Date Anyway, So Why Not?" Garlic Salsa, 50

Cousin Irene's "Happy-Holidays-from-Colorado!" Salsa, 29

Crunchy, Chewy, Sweet, and Spicy Salsa, 31

Day-After-Halloween Pumpkin Seed Salsa, 32

Desert Delight Cactus Salsa, 60

Genevieve's Berry Good Hunter-Gatherer Salsa, 37

"Get-Your-Protein" Black Bean and Roasted Corn Salsa, 38

Grandma Nannie's Cucumber Salsa, 58

Heavenly Avocado Salsa, 41

Jamaican Jerk Chicken, 53

Kay's Fit for the Gods (and Goddesses) Greek Salsa, 55

Kay's Splendid Summer Salsa, 47

Making Quesadillas, 39

Maria's "No-Crackers-Allowed" Party Salsa, 27

Peaches and Ginger Salsa, 48

Pico de Gallo Salsa, 26

Pineapple-Mango "Tropical-Paradise-in-a-Bowl" Salsa, 42

Roasted Habañero Salsa, 40

Salsa Cruda, 25

Salsa Verde, 45

Serious Chilehead Arbol-Cayenne Salsa, 44

Shelby's Boise-Style Cranberry Salsa, 51

Spicy-Sweet Melon Salsa, 49

Summer Harvest Peach, Apple, and Pear Salsa, 36

Toasting Pumpkin Seeds, 33

Torrid Thai Salsa, 46

Uncle David's Alaskan Burly Man Salsa, 28

Using that Spare Pineapple: Making Piña Coladas, 43

White Bean and Avocado Salsa for the Meek, 34

Your Basic Salsa, 24

Yummy California-Style Gingered Dessert Salsa, 59

Index to Subjects

Anaheim chili, 18
ancho chili, 18
avocadoes, 11
 Fuerte, 11
 Haas, 11
banana pepper, 19
Bermuda onions, 14
black chili. *See* pasilla chili
blender, 8
bottles, glass, 8
California chili. *See* Anaheim chili
cayenne chilies, 20
chile de arbol, 20
chile de ristra. *See* New Mexico chili
chile negro. *See* pasilla chili
chilies, 11, 17–21
 handling, 21
 roasting, 10
 storing, 21
 taming the flame, 21
Chimayo chili. *See* New Mexico chili
chipotle chili, 19
chives, 14
cilantro, 11–12
coriander seeds, 12
cucumbers, 12
 pickling, 12
cumin, 12
cutting board, 8

Dixon chili. *See* New Mexico chili
food processor, 8
Fresno chili, 18
garlic, 12
ginger, 13
grater, 8
green onions, 14
guajillo chili, 19
habañero chili, 20
Hatch chili. *See* New Mexico chili
herb chopper, 9
ingredients, some common salsa, 11–16
jalapeño chili, 19
jars, glass, 8
jicama, 13
labels, 8
lemons, 13
 reamer, 9
limes, 13
mangoes, 13
Mexican oregano, 14
mirasol chili, 19
Mulato chili, 19
New Mexico chili, 18
onions, 14
 peeling, 10
pans, 9
pasilla chili, 19
peppercorn, 14

pineapple, 15
 peeling pineapple, 15
piquin chili, 20
plum tomatoes, 16
poblano chili, 18
pots, 9
red onions, 14
roasting chilies, 10
rubber gloves, thin surgical, 9
scallions, 14
scotch bonnet chili, 20
serrano chili, 20
sesame seeds, 15
skinning (or peeling) tomatoes, 9
Spanish onions, 14
tepin chili, 20
tobasco chili, 20
tomatillos, 15
 as a replacement for green tomatoes, 15
tomatoes, 15
 skinning (or peeling) tomatoes, 9
 plum, 16
Vidalia onions, 14
white onions, 14
yellow onions, 14

64

Paraguay

Ben Box

Credits

Footprint credits
Editor: Alan Murphy
Editorial assistants: Elysia Alim, Danielle Bricker
Production and layout: Emma Bryers
Maps: Kevin Feeney

Managing Director: Andy Riddle
Commercial Director: Patrick Dawson
Publisher: Alan Murphy
Publishing Managers: Felicity Laughton, Nicola Gibbs
Digital Editors: Jo Williams, Tom Mellors
Marketing and PR: Liz Harper
Sales: Diane McEntee
Advertising: Renu Sibal
Finance and Administration: Elizabeth Taylor

Photography credits
Front cover: Pelourinho, Jose Miguel Hernandez Leon / Shutterstock
Back cover: Bitanga87 / Shutterstock

MIX
Paper from responsible sources
FSC® C013604
www.fsc.org

Printed in Great Britain by CPI Antony Rowe, Chippenham, Wiltshire

Every effort has been made to ensure that the facts in this guidebook are accurate. However, travellers should still obtain advice from consulates, airlines, etc, about travel and visa requirements before travelling. The authors and publishers cannot accept responsibility for any loss, injury or inconvenience however caused.

Publishing information
Footprint *Focus Paraguay*
1st edition
© Footprint Handbooks Ltd
September 2011

ISBN: 978 1 908206 27 5
CIP DATA: A catalogue record for this book is available from the British Library

® Footprint Handbooks and the Footprint mark are a registered trademark of Footprint Handbooks Ltd

Published by Footprint
6 Riverside Court
Lower Bristol Road
Bath BA2 3DZ, UK
T +44 (0)1225 469141
F +44 (0)1225 469461
www.footprinttravelguides.com

Distributed in the USA by Globe Pequot Press, Guilford, Connecticut

All rights reserved. No part of this publication may be reproduced, stored in a retrieval system, or transmitted, in any form or by any means, electronic, mechanical, photocopying, recording, or otherwise without the prior permission of Footprint Handbooks Ltd.

The content of Footprint *Focus Paraguay* has been taken directly from Footprint's *South American Handbook*, which was researched and written by Ben Box.

Contents

- **5 Introduction**
  - 4 *Map: Paraguay*

- **6 Planning your trip**
  - 6 Where to go
  - 8 When to go
  - 8 Getting there
  - 9 Getting around
  - 9 Sleeping
  - 9 Eating and drinking
  - 11 Essentials A-Z

- **13 Paraguay**
  - **14 Asunción**
  - 16 *Map: Asunción*
  - 19 Asunción listings
  - **31 Región Oriental: East of Asunción**
  - 34 *Map: Ciudad del Este*
  - 36 East of Asunción listings
  - **40 Iguazú Falls (Foz do Iguaçu)**
  - 41 *Map: Peruto Iguazú*
  - 43 Iguazú Falls listings
  - 47 *Map: Foz do Iguaçu*
  - 49 Foz do Iguaçu listings
  - **53 Región Oriental: South of Asunción**
  - 56 *Map: Encarnación*
  - 57 South of Asunción listings
  - **60 North of Asunción**
  - 62 North of Asunción listings
  - **64 The Chaco**
  - 69 The Chaco listings

- **73 Footnotes**
  - 74 Index

An air of mystery hangs over this under-explored pocket of South America, a country of farmland, nature and folklore. From the hot, wild impenetrable Chaco in the northwest to the lush forests of the southeast, there is abundant birdlife, a number of rivers to navigate and fantastic opportunities to experience rural tourism. Although dwarfed by its giant neighbours Brazil and Argentina, Paraguay covers some 440,000 sq km, roughly the same size as California. It is at the confluence of six eco-regions, Atlantic forest, cerrado, humid chaco, dry chaco, pantanal and pampa grasslands, resulting in a variety of landscapes and panoramas as well as rich flora and fauna.

Land-locked Paraguay has had a strange history of charismatic leaders, steadfastness and isolation. Paraguayans are proud of their Guaraní culture and heritage, evident in the widespread use of it as the officially recognized indigenous language, which is still taught in schools. Although difficult to pronounce for many outsiders, the Guaraní language cannot mask the warmth of Paraguayan hospitality. Music, too, marks Paraguay apart from its neighbours: emotive songs and European dances accompanied by virtuoso harp players and guitarists.

In other ways, Paraguay is not so separate. It shares with Argentina and Brazil remains of the mission settlements built by Jesuits near the banks of the Río Paraná, testimony to one of the major social experiments on the continent. Paraguayans are renowned for their passion for football and a dedication to a daily consumption of yerba mate (*Ilex paraguariensis*); either with ice cold water (*tereré*) on hot days, or hot water (*mate*) on cold days. Today the country is part of the Mercosur economic union, with trade routes to Argentina and Brazil well established and the road to Bolivia finally completed: the Trans-Chaco is one of the great road adventures in South America.

Planning your trip

Where to go

Paraguay is divided into two main regions separated by the Río Paraguay. The capital, **Asunción**, sits between the two; to the east of the river lies the Región Oriental (approximately 40%) and to the west the Región Occidental (approximately 60%), better known simply as the Chaco. Unless coming from Buenos Aires or Santa Cruz, it is best to plan your travels to either of these regions from Asunción.

The capital, Paraguay's largest city, has just under 600,000 inhabitants in the city proper, and sits on a bay of the Río Paraguay. The expansion of the city's metropolitan area means it now rubs shoulders with the neighbouring towns of San Lorenzo, Fernando de la Mora, Lambaré, Luque, Mariano Roque Alonso, Ñemby, San Antonio, Limpio, Capiatá and Villa Elisa. Together, these form Gran Asunción (population approximately 2.2 million). Asunción is the political and commercial heart of the country and much of its architecture dates from the early 1800s. Paraguayan history is marked by bloody wars and charismatic dictators, which is somewhat unexpected given the warmth and serenity of its people.

Región Oriental makes up most of the fertile agricultural part of the country. The towns and villages are quiet and traditional; many have unique crafts associated with them. There are also many signs of the Jesuit heritage, best exemplified at the ruins of the former mission settlements (*reducciones*) at Santísima Trinidad de Paraná and Jesús de Tavarangüé, declared World Heritage Sites by UNESCO in 1993 (along with a third, Santos Cosme y Damián), close to the city of Encarnación. From here you can cross the Río Paraná to the Argentine city of Posadas. Paraguay's eastern border with Brazil has several frontier posts, but the main one is Ciudad del Este, a duty-free shopper's paradise (or hell, depending on your point of view), where you can visit Itaipú, until recently the largest hydroelectric dam in the world. Across the Friendship Bridge from Ciudad del Este is Foz do Iguaçu in Brazil and the magnificent Iguaçu Falls.

North of Asunción there is one main town, Concepción, and the most interesting route there, if you have the time, is by river boat from the capital. The boat ride takes at least a day, so quicker ways are via the Chaco, along part of the Trans-Chaco Highway or across the Cordillera and San Pedro Departments along Ruta 3. Beyond Concepción, the Río Paraguay leads to the Brazilian Pantanal, which can also be reached by road.

Región Occidental, or Chaco makes up the western half of the country. Divided into three departments, Presidente Hayes (also known as Bajo Chaco and named after an obscure 19th century US president), Boquerón and Alto Paraguay (or Alto Chaco), the Chaco begins as a marshy palm savanna, but becomes an increasingly impenetrable and dry scrub forest as it approaches the border with Bolivia. The Trans-Chaco Highway crosses the Chaco but apart from scattered military outposts, there are few urbanized areas for 400 km until you reach the Mennonite colonies of Filadelfia, Loma Plata and Neuland which make up the Chaco Central region. A relatively short distance further northwest is the former military base of Mariscal Estigarribia. The Chaco is possibly the best place in Paraguay to see wildlife, especially birds, but you should not venture off the beaten track alone and unprepared in this part of the country.

Don't miss ...

1 **Plaza de los Héroes**, Asunción, page 16.
2 **Iguazú Falls**, page 40.
3 **Jesuit missions**, page 54.
4 **The Chaco**, page 64.

Numbers refer to the map on page 4.

National parks and nature tourism Paraguay is a confluence of globally important eco-regions and is rich in biodiversity. This abundance of wildlife is especially visible in the still largely pristine Chaco, especially in its remote national parks, along the Río Pilcomayo, and the frontier with Bolivia. Current estimates include around 7000 plant species, 100,000 invertebrates (including 765 of butterfly), 300 species of fish, 120 reptiles, 100 amphibians, 687 birds and 171 mammals. For more details, visit **Fauna Paraguay** (www.fauna paraguay.com). Paraguay has an extensive network of state-protected areas, including 12 national parks, plus two reserves, three monuments and a wildlife refuge. There are also several public-private reserves under the management of the Itaipú and Yacyretá dam companies, as well as six international protected areas. The number of private reserves has increased to 35, although unfortunately many of these protected areas exist solely on paper, and the whole system is under-funded. Visiting the protected areas is not always easy; contact the relevant institutions and authorities and never venture in without prior permission (and a good all-terrain vehicle). For a list of all 60 protected areas (public and private), visit the **Secretaría Nacional de Turismo** (www.senatur.gov.py). For state-protected areas visit **Secretaría del Ambiente** (SEAM, www.seam.gov.py). For the Itaipú and Yacyretá reserves contact the relevant environmental departments. For private reserves contact the following conservation NGOs: **Guyra Paraguay** (Gaetano Martino 215 esq Tte Ross, Asunción, T021-229097, www.guyra.org.py), which has a wealth of information for birdwatchers, naturalists and biologists as well as the capacity, infrastructure and expertise to organize tailor-made ecotours to all parts of the country, including some of the more remote locations not provided by other tour operators (highly recommended); **Fundación Moisés Bertoni para la Conservación de la Naturaleza** (Prócer Carlos Argüello 208, Asunción, T021-608740, www.mbertoni.org.py), which manages the Mbaracayú Reserve, one of the few remaining pristine Atlantic Forest reserves in the region, as well as the lesser-known Tapyta Reserve. **Desarrollo Turístico Paraguayo** (DTP, offices in Asunción and Ciudad del Este, www.dtp.com.py), the country's largest and best-known tourism agency, can organize adventure tours to different parts of the country.

When to go

The climate is sub-tropical, with a marked difference between summer and winter and often from one day to the next. December to February (summer) can be very hot and humid, with temperatures from 25° to 40°C, and even higher in the Chaco. From March to May (autumn) and September to November (spring) the heat is less oppressive, a good time for travelling. During winter (June-August) the temperature can range from 0°C at night to 28°C in the day. Temperatures below freezing are very rare, and it never snows. Some rain falls each month, but the heaviest rains tend to occur from October to April.

Getting there

Air

Most South American countries have direct flights from **Europe**; only Paraguay does not. In many cases, though, the choice of departure point is limited to Madrid and one or two other cities (Paris or Amsterdam, for instance). Argentina, Brazil and Venezuela have the most options: France, Germany, Italy, Spain and the UK (although the last named not to Venezuela). Brazil also has flights from Lisbon to a number of cities. Where there are no direct flights connections can be made in the USA (Miami, or other gateways), Buenos Aires, Rio de Janeiro or São Paulo. **Main US gateways** are Miami, Houston, Dallas, Atlanta and New York. On the west coast, Los Angeles has flights to several South American cities. If buying airline tickets routed through the USA, check that US taxes are included in the price. Flights from **Canada** are mostly via the USA, although there are direct flights from Toronto to Bogotá and Santiago. Likewise, flights from **Australia** and **New Zealand** are best through Los Angeles, except for the Qantas/LAN route from Sydney and Auckland to Santiago, and Qantas' route to Buenos Aires. From **Japan** and from **South Africa** there are direct flights to Brazil. Within **Latin America** there is plenty of choice on local carriers and some connections on US or European airlines. For airpasses, see below. To Guyana, the main routes are via the Caribbean (Port of Spain, Trinidad and Barbados) or New York, Miami and Toronto. Suriname is served by flights from Amsterdam and Port of Spain, while Guyane has flights from Paris and the French-speaking Caribbean. All three have air connections with northern Brazil.

Prices and discounts

Most airlines offer discounted fares on scheduled flights through agencies who specialize in this type of fare. For a list of these agencies see page . If you buy discounted air tickets always check the reservation with the airline concerned to make sure the flight still exists. Also remember the IATA airlines' schedules change in March and October each year, so if you're going to be away a long time it's best to leave return flight coupons open. Peak times are 7 December-15 January and 10 July-10 September. If you intend travelling during those times, book as far ahead as possible. Between February and May and September and November special offers may be available.

Sleeping and eating price codes

Sleeping
$$$$ over US$150 **$$$** US$66-150
$$ US$30-65 **$** under US$30
For a double room in high season, excluding taxes.

Eating
$$$ over US$12 **$$** US$6-12 **$** under US$6
For a two-course meal for one person, excluding drinks and service charge.

Getting around

Air There are scheduled services to most of the main parts of the country from Silvio Pettirossi airport. Domestic fares are subject to US$4 tax.

Bus Along most main roads, buses will stop at almost any junction to collect or drop off passengers, so all timetables are approximate.

Train Most of the 441-km rail network has been closed since early 2001, although freight trains continue to make sporadic trips to Encarnación, and a recently extended tourist steam train service (**Tren del Lago**) will run from Asunción, Botánico station, to Sapucaí via Areguá each Sunday (see page 28) once track repairs have finished (2011). Visit www.ferrocarriles.com.py for the latest details.

Maps A general map of the country can be purchased at most bookstores in Asunción, at bus terminals and the **Touring y Automóvil Club Paraguayo** (TACP, www.tacpy.com.py), but more detailed maps are available from **Instituto Geográfico Militar** ① *Av Artigas casi Av Perú, T021-20495*; make sure to have your passport.

Sleeping → *See box above for our hotel grade price guide.*

There are many good hotels in our **$** range, with private shower and toilet. Most hotels have two rates – one for a room with a/c, the other without. Almost all include breakfast.

Eating and drinking → *See box above for our restaurant price guide.*

Eating out Lunch is usually served between 1130-1300 in most restaurants and bars. Evening meals are hard to find in small towns, but options exist in larger cities.

Food Typical local foods include *chipa*, a cheese bread that comes in a number of varieties: *almidón*, made with yuca flour; *barrero*, made with corn flour; *manduví*, made with peanuts (better warm than cold). *Chipa so'o* is maize bread with minced meat filling; *chipa guazú* is made with fresh corn; *sopa paraguaya* is a kind of sponge of ground maize and cheese. These make a great side dish, or can be enjoyed on their own. *Soyo* is a soup of different meats and vegetables; *albóndiga* a soup of meat balls; *bori bori* another type of soup with diced meat, vegetables, and small balls of maize mixed with cheese. The beef is excellent in the better restaurants (best cuts are *lomo* and *lomito*) and can be enjoyed with *chorizo* (sausage), *morcilla, chipa guazú, sopa paraguaya* and a variety of salads. *Parrillada completa* is recommended and there are many *churrascarías* (barbecues) serving huge quantities of meat, with salad, vegetables and pasta. River fish include *surubí* and *dorado*, which are prepared in many different ways. Although vegetarian restaurants are scarce, there are lots of fruits, salads and vegetables, as well as the non-meat varieties of *empanada*, such as *choclo, palmito* or *cuatro quesos*.

Drink The most popular national drink is *tereré* (cold mate with digestive herbs) for warm days and hot mate to warm you up on cold days. *Cocido* is a type of tea made by burning (traditionally with a red ember) the yerba with some sugar; this can be served with or without milk. Paraguayan beers are very good, the better brands being *Baviera*, *Pilsen* and *Munich*. These are lager-types, but you can sometimes find darker beers in the winter. The better brands of the national sugarcane-based spirit, *caña*, include *Aristocrata* (known as 'Ari'), *Fortín* and *Tres Leones*. You can find most global brand soft drinks, including *Guaraná* (originally from Brazil). *Mosto* is a very sweet but refreshing juice from sugarcane. And there is a wonderful variety of fresh fruit juices.

Essentials A-Z

Accident and emergency
Ambulance and police emergency T911.

Electricity
220 volts AC, 50 cycles, but power surges and voltage drops are frequent. European 2 round pin plugs are used. Visitors from North America should bring an inexpensive adaptor, as few hotels outside Asunción offer 110-volt service.

Embassies and consulates
See www.embassy.goabroad.com for a full list of all Paraguayan embassies abroad, and for all foreign embassies and consulates in Paraguay.

Festivals and events
Public holidays
1 Jan; 1-3 Feb (San Blas, patron of Paraguay); 1 Mar (anniversary of the death of former president Francisco Solano López); Maundy Thu; Good Fri; 1 May (Labour Day); 15 May (Independence); 12 Jun (Paz del Chaco); 24 Jun (San Juan); 15 Aug (founding of Asunción); 16 Aug (Children's Day, in honour of the boys who died at the Battle of Acosta Ñu, see page 16); 29 Sep (victory of Boquerón, decisive battle in the Chaco War); 12 Oct (Día de la Raza); 8 Dec (Virgen de Caacupé); 25 Dec.

Internet
The average cost of internet in urban areas is US$0.75-1.25 per hour.

Money → *US$1=G3,890, €1=G5,603 (Aug 2011).*
The guaraní (plural guaraníes) is the unit of currency, symbolized by the letter G (crossed). There are bank notes for 1,000, 2,000, 5,000, 10,000, 20,000, 50,000 and 100,000 guaraníes and coins for 50, 100, 500 and 1,000 guaraníes. Get rid of all your guaraníes before leaving Paraguay; there is no market for them elsewhere (except in some *cambios* in Buenos Aires).

Plastic/TCs/banks Asunción is a good place for obtaining US$ cash on MasterCard or Visa especially if heading for Brazil. ATMs for Visa and MasterCard are common in Asunción and offer good rates of exchange. Many banks in Asunción (see page 28) give US$ cash, but charge up to 5.5% commission. Rates for most other foreign currencies are reasonable. *Casas de cambio* may want to see customers' records of purchase before accepting TCs. Visitors are advised to check on the situation on changing TCs in advance. Visa and MasterCard cash advances are possible in Asunción, Ciudad del Este and Encarnación, but only for credit (not debit) cards. Street dealers operate from early morning until late at night, even on public holidays, but double check that they are giving you the right exchange (have your own calcualtor handy).

Cost of travelling Allow US$40-50 per person per day to cover all expenses, unless staying in the cheapest hotels and not moving around much.

Opening hours
Shops, offices and businesses open around 0700; some may close 1200-1500 for lunch and siesta. **Commercial office hours** are 0730-1100 or 1300, and 1430 or 1500-1800 or 1900. **Banks**: 0845-1500, closed Sat-Sun. **Government offices**: 0700-1130 in summer, 0730-1200 in winter, open Sat.

Safety
Paraguay is generally safe and visitors are treated courteously. At election times there may be demonstrations in the capital, but the country as a whole is very calm. Beware

police seeking bribes, especially at Asunción bus station and at border crossings. See **www.policia.gov.py** for all matters related to the police and **www.mspbs.gov.py** for current health risks in Paraguay.

Tax
Airport tax US$25, payable on departure in US$ or guaraníes (cheaper).
VAT/IVA 10% (5% for some purchases).

Telephone → *Country code +595.*
Ringing: equal long tones with long pauses. Engaged: equal short tones with equal pauses. **Directory enquiries and information**: T112. Mobile phone numbers have the prefix 9, followed by 8 digits.

Time
Standard time GMT -4 hrs begins 1st Sun in Mar. Summer time GMT -3 hrs begins 2nd Sun in Oct.

Tipping
Restaurants, 10%. Porters US$0.15 per suitcase. Taxis, 10%. Porters at docks US$0.40 per suitcase. In supermarkets, tip the check-out boys who pack bags; they are not paid.

Tourist information
Secretaría Nacional de Turismo Palma 468 y 14 de Mayo, Asunción, T021-494110/441530, www.senatur.gov.py.

Useful websites
www.paraguay.gov.py Official site for general country information.
http://discoveringparaguay.com/home/ A blog about living and travelling in Paraguay.
www.cabildoccr.gov.py Centro Cultural de la República El Cabildo, the government's official cultural website (in Spanish).

www.presidencia.gov.py The government's official website (in Spanish).
www.maxicambios.com.py For currency exchange rates.
www.yagua.com Paraguayan portal with news and links.
www.abc.com.py Digital ABC (local newspaper).
www.ultimahora.com Última Hora (local newspaper).
www.lanacion.com.py La Nación (local newspaper).

Visas and immigration
A passport valid for 6 months after the intended length of stay is required to enter Paraguay and tourist visas are issued at the point of entry for a stay of up to 90 days. Visitors are registered on arrival by the immigration authorities and proof of onward travel is required (although not always asked for). Citizens of the following countries do not require visas in advance: EU member states, Israel, Japan, Norway, South Africa, Switzerland, countries of South and Central America. All others (including Australia, Canada, New Zealand and USA) must apply for a visa prior to travel, which costs £40, multiple entry £61, presenting a valid passport and 2 photos (for a business visa, a supporting letter from one's employer should suffice). Double-check at a consulate or www.mre.gov.py before arrival which nationalities need a visa and which Paraguayan consulates issue them. Make sure you're stamped in and out of Paraguay to avoid future problems. If you do not get an entrance stamp in your passport you can be turned back at the border, or have to pay a fine when leaving Paraguay.

Weights and measures
Metric.

Paraguay

Contents

14 Asunción
- 14 Ins and outs
- 15 Sights
- 16 *Map: Asunción*
- 19 Listings

31 Región Oriental: East of Asunción
- 34 *Map: Ciudad del Este*
- 36 Listings

40 Iguazú Falls (Foz do Iguaçu)
- 41 *Map: Peruto Iguazú*
- 43 Listings
- 46 Brazil side of the falls
- 47 *Map: Foz do Iguaçu*
- 49 Listings

53 Región Oriental: South of Asunción
- 56 *Map: Encarnación*
- 57 Listings

60 North of Asunción
- 62 Listings

64 The Chaco
- 69 Listings

At a glance

↻ **Time required** 1-3 weeks.

❄ **Best time** Sep/Oct and Mar-May are not too hot or wet.

✖ **When not to go** Heaviest rains Nov-Mar; Dec-Feb can be excessively hot.

Asunción

Asunción was founded in 1537 on the eastern bank of a calm bay in the Río Paraguay. It is the longest continually inhabited area in the River Plate Basin and is sometimes referred to as the "Mother of Cities" because it was from here that colonial expeditions set off to establish other cities. The centre is a testament to 19th-century ideals, with names reflecting its heroes and battles. Tree-lined avenues, parks and squares break up the rigid grid system. In July and August the city is drenched in colour with the prolific pink bloom of the lapacho trees, which grow everywhere.

Ins and outs → *Phone code: 021. Population: 589,000 (city); 2.2 million (urban area).*

Getting there Silvio Pettirossi International **airport** is in Luque, 16 km northeast of the city centre, from which taxis, buses and an airport-to-hotel minibus service run. It takes from 30-45 minutes from the airport to town. The **bus terminal** is south of the centre, also 30-45 minutes away. You can go by taxi or by city bus (see page 26 for the correct one). Both the airport and bus terminal have tourist information desks. ▸▸ *See also Transport, page 26.*

Getting around Most of the historical sights of interest are in a relatively small area by the river, so walking between them is not a problem. Similarly, there are many central hotels within walking distance of these sights. Places outside this zone are easily reached by taxi or bus. If going by taxi, give driver the specific street address but also the name of the nearest intersection. Almost all locations in Asunción are referred to in this manner. Note also that the often-used "casi" (near) and "esquina" both generally mean "at the corner of". The bus system is extensive and runs 0600-2400; buses stop at signs before every street corner. Asunción is very spread out and transport so slow that you need to allow 60-90 minutes to get beyond its limits.

Tourist offices Secretaría Nacional de Turismo ⓘ *Palma 468, T494110/441530, Mon-Fri 0800-1300 (phone Mon-Sat 0800-1900 for information).* Good free map (ask for it), information on all parts of Paraguay, but you may need to be persistent. Other maps are sold in bookshops. Information on Asunción at www.asu-cvb.org.py (Spanish and English). The city of Asunción's municipal web site ⓘ *www.mca.gov.py* also has excellent, up-to-date information in Spanish.

Sights → *For listings, see pages 19-30.*

Historic centre

At the bottom of Avenida Colón, just before it joins El Paraguayo Independiente, are the colonial façades of **La Recova**, shops selling local arts and crafts. The main river port and **Aduana** (Customs) are at this same junction. Continue along El Paraguayo Independiente to a small plaza on your left with a statue of the former dictator, Alfredo Stroessner. After his deposition, the statue was crushed and placed inside a block of concrete, only his hands and face protruding. Next to this is the **Palacio de Gobierno**, built in the style of Versailles by Alan Taylor as a palace for Francisco Solano López (1860-1869). During the later years Taylor was forced to use child labour as all adult men were enlisted to fight in the Triple Alliance War. It now houses government departments. Down the side of the palace towards the river is a platform for viewing the back of the building. Directly opposite the Palace is the **Manzana de la Rivera** ⓘ *Ayolas 129 y El Paraguayo Independiente, T445085, Mon-Sat 0700-2000, library Mon-Fri 0700-1900, Sat 0800-1200*, nine restored buildings and a patio area dating from 1700s including **Casa Viola** with Museo Memoria de la Ciudad with historical photos and city information, **Casa Clari**, with exhibition halls and a bar, and **Casa Vertua**, the municipal library. These collectively represent the most complete set of colonial era buildings in the city.

Next to the Palace is the **Congreso Nacional**, built in steel and glass representing a huge ship moored on the river bank and incorporating part of the old congress building. On **Plaza de la Independencia** (often referred to as Plaza Constitución or Plaza Juan de Salazar) there is a small memorial to those who died in the struggle for democracy (also look out for statues of the frog and the dog). On the Plaza are the **Antiguo Colegio Militar** (1588) originally a Jesuit College, now home to government ministries, the **Cabildo** ⓘ *Mon-Fri 0900-1900, Sat 0800-1200, free*, now the **Centro Cultural de la República**, with temporary exhibitions, indigenous and religious art, museum of music, film and video on the top floor, and the **Catedral Metropolitana** (mid-17th century, rebuilt in the mid-19th century) ⓘ *not always open, but hours posted in front, possible to view the interior before, after or during mass, usually around 1100 daily*. The altar, decorated with Jesuit and Franciscan silver, is very beautiful. From the Plaza turn right onto Alberdi and to your right is the **Correos** (post office), a colonial building with a lovely planted courtyard and a small museum; it also has public toilets. At Alberdi and Presidente Franco is the **Teatro Municipal Ignacio Pane** ⓘ *T448820, www.teatromunicipal.com.py, for information on events*, fully restored to its former *Belle Époque* glory. The **Estación San Roque** ⓘ *Ayala y México, just below Plaza Uruguaya, T447848,* was built in 1856 with British and European help. Paraguay had the first passenger carrying railway in South America. No trains now run from the station, but it has a small **museum** ⓘ *0700-1200, free*, featuring the old ticket office, machinery from Wolverhampton and Battersea and the first steam engine in Paraguay, the Sapucaí (1861). **Plaza Uruguaya**, at the nexus of Calles México, Eligio Ayala, 25 de Mayo and Antequera, with its shady trees and fountain is another spot to stop and rest. From here take Mariscal Estigarribia towards Plaza de Los Héroes. The **Museo Nacional de Bellas Artes** ⓘ *Mcal Estigarribia e Iturbe, T447716, www.portalguarani.com/ detalles_museos.php?id=3, Tue-Fri 0700-1900, Sat 0700-1200, closed Sun-Mon,* has some interesting 20th-century Paraguayan art and a good small collection of European paintings including works by Tintoretto and Murrillo.

Mariscal Estigarribia becomes Palma at the intersection with Independencia Nacional (the names of all streets running east to west change at this point). On **Plaza de los Héroes** is the **Panteón Nacional de los Héroes** ⓘ *Palma y Chile, open daily*, which is based on Les Invalides in Paris, begun during the Triple Alliance War and finished in 1937. It contains the tombs of Carlos Antonio López, Mariscal Francisco Solano López, Mariscal Estigarribia, the victor of the Chaco War, an unknown child-soldier, and other national heroes. The child-soldiers honoured in the Panteón were boys aged 12-16 who fought at the battle of Acosta Ñu in the War of the Triple Alliance, 15 August 1869. Most of the boys died and somewhere between 60%-70% of adult Paraguayan men were killed during the war. Sight-seeing here is strictly on your own. Plaza de los Héroes is made up of four separate squares with different names but these are very rarely used; it is sometimes referred to as Plaza de la Democracia.

On the Plaza at Chile y Oliva (Plaza Libertad) there are **covered market stalls** selling traditional Paraguayan arts and crafts in wood, cotton and leather. Along Palma indigenous women sell colourful woven bags, beads and baskets. You may be approached by

Asunción

Sleeping
1 Adelia *C6*
2 Amalfi *C4*
3 Aspen Apart Hotel *C1*
4 Asunción Palace *B1*
5 Bavaria *B6*
6 Black Cat Hostel *A3*
7 Cardel *C6*
8 Cecilia *B6*
9 Chaco *B4*
10 City *C3*
11 El Lapacho *A6*
12 Excelsior *C3*
13 Granados Park & Restaurants Bistro & Estrella *B2*
14 Gran Armele *B1*
15 La Española *C4*
16 Paramanta *A6*
17 Portal del Sol *A6*
18 Res Itapúa *C6*
19 Sabe Center *B4*
20 Sheraton *A6*
21 Westfalenhaus *A6*
22 Yasy *C6*

16 • Paraguay Asunción sights

indigenous men selling whistles, bows and arrows or feather headdresses. A few blocks further along Palma is the **tourist information office**; it has craft stalls for those not wishing to buy on the street. On Saturday morning, till 1200, Palma becomes a pedestrian area, with stalls selling arts, crafts, clothes and during the summer there is entertainment outside the tourist office. On Sunday there are stalls selling second-hand or antique items around Plaza de los Héroes. From Palma turn right at 14 de Mayo to the **Casa de la Independencia** ① *14 de Mayo y Pdte Franco, www.casa delaindependencia.org.py, Mon-Fri 0700-1830, Sat 0800-1200, free* (1772), with a historical collection; the 1811 anti-colonial revolution was plotted here. The **Iglesia de Encarnación** ① *14 de Mayo y Víctor Haedo*, partially restored after a fire in 1889 by an Italian immigrant who offered his services gratis on condition that he be free to select the best materials, in spite of its obvious need for immediate restoration again, is a tranquil place to end your tour.

Heading out of the centre along Avenida Mariscal López

The **Museo Histórico Militar** ① *in the Ministry of National Defence, Mcal López y 22 de Septiembre (surrender passport on entry), Mon-Fri 0700-1300, free*, has articles from both the Triple Alliance and the Chaco Wars. These include blood-stained flags from the Triple Alliance as well as clothes and personal possessions of Franciso Solano López and his Irish mistress, Eliza Lynch. The national cemetery, **Cementerio Recoleta** ① *Av Mcal López y Chóferes del Chaco*, resembles a miniature city with tombs in various architectural styles. It contains the tomb of Madame Lynch (ask guide to show you the location), and, separately, the tomb of her baby daughter Corrine (Entrada 3 opposite Gran Unión supermarket). Eliza Lynch's home at the corner of Yegros and Mariscal Estigarribia was, until 1999, the Facultad de Derecho.

On the southeast outskirts of Asunción is **San Lorenzo** (Km 12). Reached via Ruta 2 (Mariscal Estigarribia Highway) or take buses 12, 56, 26 and get off at central plaza with blue, 18th-century neo-Gothic cathedral. The **Museo Guido Boggiani** ① *Bogado 888 y Saturio Ríos, T584717, 1½ blocks from plaza, daily until 1900, ring the bell if door is shut*, is staffed by a very helpful lady who explains the exhibits, which include rare Chamacoco feather art,

Eating
1 Bolsi *B3*
2 Dali *B2*
3 El Mirasol *B4*
4 El Molino *B2*
5 La Flor de la Canela *A5*
6 La Vida Verde *B2*
7 Le Saint Tropez *B4*
8 Lido *B3*
9 Metropol *B6*
10 Oliver's (Hotel Presidente) *C3*
11 San Roque *B5*
12 Taberna Española *C1*

Bars & clubs
13 Britannia Pub *B5*

and a well-displayed collection of tribal items from the northern Chaco from the turn of the 20th century. The shop across the road sells crafts at good prices. There's also a small Museo Arqueológico near the church and a daily market. The **Facultad de Ciencias Agrarias** ⓘ *on the campus of the Universidad Nacional de Asunción, Mon-Fri 0800-1530, closed Jan, free*, has an interesting small museum with natural history collections. Ask guard at gate for directions.

Heading out of the centre along Avenida España

Museo Etnográfico Dr Andrés Barbero ⓘ *España 217 y Mompox, T441696, www.museo barbero.org.py, Mon-Fri 0700-1100, Mon, Wed, Fri 1500-1700, free*, houses a good collection of tools and weapons of the various Guaraní cultures. The Centro de Artes Visuales includes the **Museo del Barro** – the most popular museum in the country by far – and the **Museo de Arte Indígena** ⓘ *Grabadores del Cabichuí entre Cañada y Emeterio Miranda, T607996, exhibitions open Thu-Sat, 1530-2000, US$2.50, free on Fri, shop and café Wed-Sat 1530-2000, take bus 30 or 44A from the centre past Shopping del Sol, ask driver for Cañada*. Contains both contemporary and indigenous art, outstanding displays of rarely seen colonial art, bookshop, café. Highly recommended.

    Luque (take bus 30), founded 1636, has an attractive central plaza with some well-preserved colonial buildings and a pedestrianized area with outdoor cafes. It is famous for the making of Paraguayan harps and guitars (**Guitarras Sanabria** ⓘ *Km 13, T21-2291, www.arpasgsanabria. com.py*, is one of the best-known firms), and for fine filigree jewellery in silver and gold at very good prices, many shops on the main street. Tourist information at Plaza General Aquino. There are some fine musical instrument shops on the road to Luque along Av Aviadores del Chaco.

Other sights

The best of several parks is **Parque Carlos Antonio López**, set high to the west along Colón and, if you can find a gap in the trees, with quite a grand view. Another place for good views is **Cerro de Lambaré**, 7 km south (buses 9 and 29 from Gral Díaz).

    Six kilometres east, the 250-ha **Jardín Botánico** ⓘ *Av Artigas y Primer Presidente, www.mca. gov.py/zoo.htm, 0700-1700 daily, US$0.45*, lies along the Río Paraguay, on the former estate of the López family. The gardens are well-maintained, with signed walks and a rose garden, and are bordered by the 18-hole Asunción Golf Club. In the gardens are the former residences of Carlos Antonio López, a one-storey typical Paraguayan country house with verandas, now housing a **Museo de Historia Natural** and a library, and of Solano López, a two-storey European-inspired mansion which is now the **Museo Indigenista** (neither in good condition). ⓘ *Both museums are free, Mon-Sat 0730-1130, 1300-1730, Sun 0900-1300. Getting there: by bus (Nos 2, 6, 23, and 40, US$0.15, 35 mins from Luis A Herrera, or Nos 24, 35 or 44B from Oliva or Cerro Corá)*. The church of **Santísima Trinidad** (on Santísimo Sacramento, parallel to Avenida Artigas), where Carlos Antonio López was originally buried, dating from 1854 with frescoes on the inside walls, is well worth a visit. Nearby is the wreck of the **Ycuá Bolaños supermarket** ⓘ *Santísima Trinidad y Artigas*, which was destroyed by fire in August 2004, killing 396 people when the doors were ordered locked by the owners (now in jail) to prevent looting. It is now a memorial with a donation box for the families of the dead. The **Maca indigenous community** ⓘ *US$0.40, guide US$0.65, take bus 42 or 44*, is just north of the Botanical Gardens. The *indígenas* live in poor conditions and expect you to photograph them (US$0.15).

Around Asunción

Many villages close to Asunción can be visited on a day trip: eg Areguá and San Bernadino on Lago Ypacari (see page 32), Altos, great views over the lake, Itauguá (traditional lace and handicrafts centre). Alternatively take a tour from any travel agent (see Activities and tours, page 24) of the **Circuito de Oro**: destinations vary but tend to include Itá, Yaguarón, Paraguarí, Piribebuy, Caacupé, San Bernardino, Areguá, Itauguá, 200 km on paved roads, seven hours. The route goes through the rolling hills of the Cordillera, no more than 650 m high, which are beautiful, with hidden waterfalls and a number of spas: Chololó, Piraretá (near Piribebuy) and Pinamar (between Piribebuy and Paraguarí) are the most developed. The **Camino Franciscano** is similar, including the historical towns of Ypané, Altos, Itá, Atyra, Yaguarón, Piribebuy, Tobatí, Caacupé, Valenzuela, Villarrica, Caazapá and San Juan Neopomuceno.

Asunción listings

For Sleeping and Eating price codes and other relevant information, see pages 9-10.

Sleeping

The hotel bill does not usually include a service charge. Look out for special offers. For Asunción's **Sheraton ($$$$)**, see www.sheraton-asuncion.com.py.

Asunción *p15, map p16*

$$$$ Granados Park, Estrella y 15 de Agosto, T497921, www.granadospark.com.py. Luxury, top quality hotel, range of suites with breakfast, all facilities, Wi-Fi, good restaurant *Il Mondo*.

$$$$ Hotel Casino Yacht y Golf Club Paraguayo, 14 km from town, at Lambaré, on own beach on the Río Paraguay, T906121, www.resortyacht.com.py. 7 restaurants and cafés, super luxury, with pool, gym, spa, golf, tennis, airport transfers; many extras free, special deals.

$$$$ Sabe Center, 25 de Mayo y México, T450093, www.sabecenterhotel.com.py. Luxury hotel in modern tower, with all facilities, discounts available.

$$$ Aspen Apart Hotel, Ayolas 581 y Gral Díaz, T496066, www.aspen.com.py. Modern, lots of marble, 50 suites and apartments, with breakfast, pool, sauna, gym, internet, cheaper longer stays.

$$$ Cecilia, Estados Unidos 341 y Estigarribia, T210365, www.hotelcecilia.com.py. Comfortable suites, breakfast included, weekend specials, internet, good restaurant, *La Preferida* (**$$$**), pool with a view, sauna, gym, airport transfers, parking, medical service.

$$$ Chaco, Caballero 285 y Estigarribia, T492066, www.hotelchaco.com.py. Central 1970s hotel, with breakfast, parking nearby, rooftop swimming pool, Wi-Fi, internet, bar, good restaurant (**$$$**).

$$$ Excelsior, Chile 980, T495632, www.excelsior.com.py. Luxurious, stylish, gym, pool, tennis, internet, cell phone rental, bar and restaurant.

$$$ Hotel Westfalenhaus, Sgto 1° M Benítez 1577 C Santísima Trinidad, T292374, www.paraguay-hotels.com. Comfortable, German-run, breakfast included, half board, weekly rates and self-catering apartments available, with pool, Wi-Fi, safe deposit box, a/c, international restaurant, *Piroschka*, gym, massage and spa, English, German and Spanish spoken.

$$$ Paramanta, Av Aviadores del Chaco 3198, T607053, www.paramanta-hotel.com. 4-star, mid-way between airport and centre, buses stop outside, with breakfast, TV, Wi-Fi internet, bar, restaurant, pool, gym, gardens, and many other services. English and German spoken.

$$ Amalfi, Caballero 877 esq Fulgencio R Moreno y Manuel Domínguez, T494154, www.hotel amalfi.com.py. Modern, comfortable, spacious rooms, breakfast included, internet and restaurant. Recommended.
$$ Asunción Palace, Colón 415 y Estrella, T492153, www.geocities.com/aphotel. Historic building dating from 1858. 24 rooms, with breakfast, a/c, TV, fridge, very helpful, elegant, laundry, internet.
$$ Bavaria, Chóferes del Chaco 1010, T600966, www.hotel-bavaria-py.com. Comfortable, colonial style, beautiful garden, pool, a/c, good value rooms and suites with kitchens, TV, fridge, German spoken, very helpful staff.
$$ City Hotel, Humaitá 209 y NS de la Asunción, T491497, www.cityhotel.com.py. A/c, good, with breakfast in City Cafetería in lobby.
$$ Gran Armele, Palma 999 y Colón, T444455, www.hotelarmele.com.py. With breakfast, a/c, gym, sauna, restaurant, Wi-Fi, pool, large hotel used by tour groups.
$$ El Lapacho, República Dominicana 543 casi Av España, T210662, www.lapacho. com.py. Family-run, welcoming, comfortable, a bit run down, rooms available at lower prices. Favourite with backpackers and students. Convenient for local services, 10 mins from centre by bus, pool, 24-hr internet, parking.
$$ Portal del Sol, Av Denis Roa 1455 y Santa Teresa, T609395, www.hotelportaldelsol.com. Comfortable hotel with breakfast, some rooms sleep 4, free airport pick-up and Wi-Fi, internet, pool.
$ pp Black Cat Hostel, Eligio Ayala 129 casi Independencia Nacional, T449827, www.hostelblackcat.com. Central backpacker hostel with dorms and private rooms (**$$**), helpful with travel advice, breakfast included, internet and Wi-Fi, use of kitchen, good location.

$ Cardel, Ygurey 1145 and Av Dr. Eusebio Alaya, T213622, cardel@highway.com.py. Halfway between bus station and centre of town, breakfast included.
$ La Española, Herrera 142 y F Yegros, T449280, www.hotellaespanola.galeon.com. Central, comfortable, breakfast included, a/c, internet access, credit cards accepted, airport pick-up, laundry, luggage storage, restaurant, parking. Recommended.
$ Residencial Itapúa, Fulgencio R Moreno 943, T445121. Breakfast available at small cost, a/c, cheaper with fan, kitchen for drinks and snacks, no cooking, quiet, comfortable.

Near the bus terminal
$ Adelia, Av F de la Mora y Rep Argentina y Lapacho, T553083. With breakfast, modern, TV a/c.
$ Yasy, Av F de la Mora 2390, T551623. A/c and TV, cheaper with fan; both are overpriced.

Many more behind these in Calle Dolores; many others in same class near bus station.

Out of the city: San Lorenzo
Estancia Oñondivemi, Tourism farm, Km 27.5 on Ruta 1 just past the turn off to Ruta 2 at San Lorenzo, 30 mins from Asunción, T0295-20344 or 9-8144 1460, www.onondivemi.com.py. A pleasant escape from the city. Serves all meals, food organically grown on site. Horse riding, fishing, swimming, nature walks (they have a nearby property with a waterfall, lovely for swimming), attractive accommo dation with a/c. Groups welcome. Contact for prices (includes meals).
Camping If camping, take plenty of insect repellent. The pleasant site at the **Jardín Botánico** is US$2.50 pp plus tent, cars also permitted, cold showers and 220v electricity, busy at weekends.

You can camp at rear of **Restaurant Westfalia**, Av Perón y Av F Bogado, T331772, www.westfalia-paraguay.com.

Owner speaks English, French, German, knowledgeable, US$2 per night for car, showers, laundry, noisy, animals. Take Av General Santos, towards Lambaré. Restaurant Westfalia is 5 km from Asunción (bus 19, 23 or 40).

Eating

Asunción *p15, map p16*
Many restaurants are outside the scope of the map. A few restaurants close at weekends, but may open at night. A good meal in the food halls at the shopping malls, which you pay for by weight, as you do in some of the city centre restaurants, is about US$3.25. Average price of a good meal in quality restaurants: US$20-24. The following are open most days of the week, day and night.

$$$ Acuarela, Mcal López casi San Martín, T601750. Very good churrascaría and other Brazilian dishes.
$$$ Bistro, 15 de Agosto y Estrella, T497921. In **Granados Park Hotel**, excellent, US$30.
$$$ Bolsi, Estrella 399 y Alberdi, T491841. One of Asunción's longest-operating eateries. Enormously popular. Wide choice of wines, good for breakfast, excellent food (Sun 1200-1430) in large servings. Has great diner next door, lower prices, also popular.
$$$ Churrasquería Sajón, Av Carlos A López, bus 26 from centre. Good Paraguayan harp/guitar group; restaurant serving meat.
$$$ Fabio Rolandi's, Mcal López y Infante Rivarola, T610447. Delicious pasta, steak and fish. Recommended.
$$$ Fina Estampa, Senador Long 789 y Tte Vera, T601686, www.finaestampa.com.py. Peruvian food. Good Sun lunch buffet.
$$$ La Pergola Jardín, Perú 240 y José Bergés, T214014. Under the same ownership as Bolsi, excellent.
$$$ Le Saint Tropez, México 466 entre Cerro Corrá y 25 de Mayo, T441141, lesainttropez@yahoo.com. Recently remodeled and under new ownership.

Beautiful setting. Bar and restaurant, pizzería, open for lunch and dinner
$$$ Mburicao, González Rioobó 737 y Chaco Real, T660048. Mediterranean food. Highly recommended.
$$$ Oliver's, Hotel Presidente, Azara e Independencia Nacional, T494941. Very good, pricey, live music.
$$$ Shangrila, Aviadores del Chaco y San Martín, T661618. Very good food at upmarket Chinese.
$$$ Sukiyaki, in Hotel Uchiyamada, Constitución 763 y Luis A de Herrera, T222038. Good Japanese, about US$12 pp.
$$$ Taberna Española, Ayolas 631 y General Díaz, T441743. Spanish food, very good.
$$ Dali, Estrella 695 y Juan E. O' Leary, T490890. Snack-bar-style eatery. Good Italian (and other) food, nice terrace. Recommended.
$$ Hacienda Las Palomas, Guido Spano y Senador Long 644, T605111. Mexican food, popular.
$$ Hiroshima, Chóferes del Chaco 1803 y Av Moreno, T662945. Authentic Japanese.
$$ Lido, Plaza de los Héroes, Palma y Chile, T446171. Open daily 0700-2300. An institution in Asunción, great location across from Panteón, loads of character. Good for breakfast, empanadas and watching the world go by. Good quality and variety, famous for fish soup, delicious, very popular. Recommended.
$$ San Roque, Eligio Ayala y Tacuary, T446015. Traditional, relatively inexpensive.
$$-$ Paulista Grill, San Martín casi Mcal López, T662185, www.paulistagrill.com.py. Another good churrascaría, good value, cheaper in the week, popular with groups.
$ El Cheff Peruano, General Garay 431 y Del Maestro, T605756, www.elchef peruano.com. Good quality Peruvian food, also popular with large groups.
$ El Mirasol, 25 de Mayo 241, entre Yegros e Iturbe. Open till 1600 for buffet lunch, closed Sun. Vegetarian and Chinese.

$ La Vida Verde, Palma 634 y 15 de Agosto, T446611. Open till 1700, closed Sun. Vegetarian, Chinese influenced, with buffet lunch, .
$ Tapei, Tte Fariña 1049 y Brasil y Estados Unidos, T201756. Serves stylish vegetarian by weight. Recommended.
$ Tembi'u he, Dr Francisco Fernández y Av Santísima Trinidad, T293324. Paraguayan food.

Cafés and snacks
Most cheap lunch places close around 1600.
Café Literario, Mcal Estigarribia 456, T491640. Mon-Fri from 1600. Cosy café/bar, books and good atmosphere. Occasional cultural events with Alianza Francesa.
El Molino, España 382 y Brasil, T225351, www.confiteriaelmolino.com. Good value, downstairs for sandwiches and homemade pastries, upstairs for full meals in a nice setting, good service and food (particularly steaks) but pricey. Bakery as well. Recommended. Second location at Oliva y 14 de Mayo, T491436.
Estrella, Estrella y 15 de Agosto. In Granados Park Hotel, pizza, *empanadas*.
Heladería París, 3 locations: Brasilia y Siria, San Martín y Pacheco and NS de Asunción y Quinta Avenida. Café/bar/ice cream parlour. Popular.
La Flor de la Canela, Tacuary 167 y Eligio Ayala, T498928. Cheap Peruvian lunches.
Metropol, Estados Unidos 341 y 25 de Mayo, T202222, www.hotelcecilia.com.py/mp/menu.php. Café and shop with European food, sandwiches, cheese and meats. Part of **Hotel Cecilia**.
Michael Bock, Pres Franco 828, T495847. Excellent bread and sweet shop, specializing in German pastries.
Quattro D (4d), San Martín y Dr Andrade, T497604. Ice cream parlour offering great range of flavours, also weekday lunches from US$1.85.
Sugar's, several branches including most Shopping Centres and Brasilia 662.

Bars and clubs

Asunción *p15, map p16*
Bars
The best up to date online source for bars and clubs in Asunción, Ciudad del Este and anywhere else in Paraguay is www.asunfarra.com.py.
Britannia Pub, Cerro Corá 851, T443990, www.britannia-pub.com. Evenings only, closed Mon. Good variety of drinks, German spoken, popular expat hangout, book exchange.
Café Bohemia Senador Long 848 casi España, T662191. Original decor and atmosphere, Mon and Tue live blues/jazz, alternative at weekends.
Déjà Vu, Galería Colonial, Av España casi San Rafael, T615098. Popular.
Paseo Carmelitas, Av Espana y Malutin, tiny but upscale mall has several popular bars, such as **El Bar**, **Kamastro**, **Kilkenney Irish Pub**, **Liquid** and the very chic **Sky Resto & Lounge** (T600940, www.skylounge.com.py) as well as restaurants and shops.
Refuel, Galería Colonial, Av España casi San Rafael. Yet another popular bar, more upscale than most and with live music nightly.

Clubs
Av Brasilia has a collection of clubs such as **Arena & Café, Ristretto Café & Bar** (No 671 y Siria, T224614) and **Mouse Cantina** (No 803 y Patria, T 228794).
Asunción Rock, Mcal Estigarribia 991 y Estados Unidos, T442034. Wed-Sat, 2200 till late. 2 dance floors, rock and alternative music.
Coyote Night & Fun, Sucre casi Av San Martín, T622816, www.coyote.com.py. Fri, Sat. Several dance floors and bars, retractable roof, affluent crowd, see website for other events in different locations including Ciudad del Este and San Bernardino. Recommended.
El Sitio Disco, Av Rep Argentina 1035 y McMahon, T612822. Fri-Sat, 2100 till 0300. Latin and retro,

Face's, Av Mcal López 2585 (technically in Fernando de la Mora), T671421/672768, www.faces.com.py. Also in Ciudad del Este. Largest club in Paraguay, shows nightly.

Glam, Av San Martin 1155 y Agustín Barrios, T331905, www.glam.com.py. Thu, Fri and Sat. Along with Coyote and Face's (see above), one of Asunción's most popular clubs. Same owners as **Caracol Club**, Av Perón y Concepción Yegros, T332848, www.caracol.com.py. Electronic music, several dance floors, 20 min drive from centre.

Pirata Bar, Benjamín Constant y Ayolas, T452953, www.piratabar.com.py. Fri-Sat, 2100 till 0300.

Trauma, 25 de Mayo y Antequera y Tacuary. Fri, Sat, 2300. Gay/transvestite/mixed.

Entertainment

Asunción *p15, map p16*

Cinema Cinema programmes are given in the press; latest releases, admission US$4.75 (Wed and matinées half price). Modern cinemas at: **Shopping del Sol**, 6 screens, **Shopping Villa Mora** 6 screens, and **Mall Excelsior**, **Hiperseis** (see Supermarkets and shopping centres, below). **Centro Cultural de la Ciudad**, Haedo 347, T442448, for quality foreign films, US$1.50.

Theatre See newspapers for performances of concerts, plays, ballets. Various Cultural centres also put on theatrical productions. For online listings, check **ABC Digital** (www.abc.com.py), **Última Hora** (www.ultimahora.com) and **La Nación** (www.lanacion.com.py). **Teatro Municipal**, Alberdi y Pdte Franco, T445169, www.mca.gov.py/teatrom.html. Ticket sales Mon-Sat 0800-2200. **Banco Central**, T6192243, the Paraguay Philharmonic gives monthly recitals May-Dec. **Teatro de las Américas**, J Bergés 297, concerts are given here.

Festivals and events

Asunción *p15, map p16*
Two weeks in **Jul**, **Expo**, an annual trade show at Mariano Roque Alonso, Km 14.5 on the Trans-Chaco Highway, www.expo.com.py. The biggest fair in the country with local and international exhibitors. Packed at weekends. Bus from centre takes 30 mins.

Shopping

Asunción *p15, map p16*
Bookshops English-language books are expensive throughout Paraguay. Better prices and selections are had in Argentina and Brazil. **'Books'**, at Shopping del Sol and Mcal López 3971, also opposite Villa Morra shopping centre, very good for English books, new titles and classics. **El Lector** at Plaza Uruguaya y 25 de Mayo, T491966, also at San Martín y Austria, T614256 (has café and internet connection), www.ellector.com.py. Has a selection of foreign material and a range of its own titles on Paraguay. **Librería Alemana**, Av Luis A de Herrera 292, warmly recommended for German books. **Librería Internacional**, Oliva 386, Estrella 723 and Palma 595. Good for maps, indigenous cultures; sometimes sponsors concerts and recitals in stores.

Camping Camping 44, Av Artigas 2061, T297240, www.camping44.com.py (also fishing and hunting supplier); **Gauchito Deportes**, Av Fernando de la Mora 2477 y Cedro, T555953, or **Unicentro**, Palma y 15 de Agosto; Nueva Americana, Mcal Estigarribia 111 esq Independencia Nacional, T492021, www.nuevaamericana.com.py.

Crafts Check the quality of all handicrafts carefully, lower prices usually mean lower quality. Many leading tourist shops offer up to 15% discount for cash; many others will not accept credit cards, so ask even if there are signs in window saying they do. For leather goods there are several places on Colón and on Montevideo including:

Boutique Irene, No 463; **Boutique del Cuero**, No 329; and **Galería Colón 185** (recommended). Also **La Casa del Portafolio**, Av Palma 302, T558228.
Artes de Madera at Ayolas 222. Wooden articles and carvings. **Casa Overall 1**, Mcal Estigarribia y Caballero, T448657, good selection. Also **No 2** at 25 de Mayo y Caballero, T447891. **Casa Vera**, Estigarribia 470, T445868, for Paraguayan leatherwork, cheap and very good. **Doña Miky**, O'Leary 215 y Pres Franco, recommended. **Folklore**, Mcal Estigarribia e Iturbe, T/F494360, good for music, woodcarvings and other items. **Victoria**, **Arte Artesanía**, Iturbe y Ayala, T450148, interesting selection of wood carvings, ceramics etc. Recommended.
Electronic goods Cheap electronic goods in the Korean-run shops along Palma.
Markets Mercado Cuatro on Pettirossi, a huge daily market selling food, clothing, electrical items, DVDs, CDs, jewellery, toys, is a great place to visit. Good, cheap Chinese restaurants nearby. There is a daily market on Av Dr Francia, best visited during the week. See also under Historic centre, Sights. **Shopping Mariscal López** (see below) has a fruit and vegetable market, Tue, in the car park, and a small plant/flower market, including orchids, Wed, at the entrance.
Shopping centres Asunción has a number of modern Shopping Malls with shops, ATMs, cafés, supermarkets, cinemas and food halls all under one a/c roof. Most also offer Wi-Fi coverage. **Shopping Villa Morra** (Av Mcal López y San Roque González, T603050, www.shoppingvillamorra.com.py). **Shopping Mariscal López** (Quesada 5050 y Charles de Gaulle, behind Shopping Villa Morra, T611272, www.mariscallopez.com.py). **Shopping del Sol** (Av Aviadores de Chaco y D F de González, T611780, www.delsol.com.py). **Mall Excelsior** (Chile y Manduvirá, T443015, www.mallexcelsior.com).
Supermarkets Hiperseis at Boggiani y Mcal López; **Stock** at Shopping del Sol and Mall Excelsior. **Superseis** at Shopping Villa Morra; **Casa Rica**, Av San Martín y Aviadores del Chaco, good for speciality foods and some European imports. **Real Villa Mora**, Boggiani y Av Argentina, has an imported food aisle, mainly from USA.

▲ Activities and tours

Asunción *p15, map p16*
Football Asunción (technically next-door Luque) is the permanent home of the **South American Football Confederation**, CONMEBOL (www.conmebol.com), on the autopista heading towards the airport, opposite Ñu Guazú Park. This imposing building with its striking 'football' fountain houses offices, a hall of fame, extensive football library and a new museum with interactive exhibits, T494628 in advance for visits. See also **Asociación Paraguaya de Futbol**, www.apf.org.py. **Estadio Defensores del Chaco**, Mayor Martínez 1393 y Alejo García, T480120, is the national stadium, hosting international, cup and major club matches.
Horse riding Club Hípico Paraguayo, Av Eusebio Ayala y Benjamín Aceval, Barrio San Jorge Mariano Roque Alonso, T756148. Actually 9 different athletic clubs in one; scene of many Asunción society events. Members club (US$55 per month but daily rates available) open to the public. Friendly and helpful.
Nature tourism See page 7.
Rural tourism *Turismo rural* has become one of the most enjoyable ways to visit the country and get a feel for a Paraguayan way of life that revolves around agriculture and ranching. Although not as advanced as rural tourism in Argentina or Uruguay, the sector is growing in Paraguay, particularly in the southeast (in Paraguarí, Caaguazú, Guairá and Caazapá departments) and to the north of Asunción (in Cordillera and San Pedro departments). The **Touring y Automóvil Club Paraguayo** (25 de Mayo y Brasíl, p 2,

T210550, www.tacpy.com.py) an excellent source of information on rural tourism, both through the **Paraguayan Rural Tourism Association** (APATUR), Don Bosco 881, T497028, www.apatur.org.py, and its own travel agency, **Touring Viajes**. They organize visits to ranches and farms all over Paraguay. One-day tour prices start at about US$60 pp including accommodation, food and drink (not alcohol); tours of three or more days for groups of 2-12, US$80-150. All the ranches listed under APATUR have good facilities. Transport to and from these ranches from Asunción is sometimes included in the package. Visitors experience living and working on a ranch, can participate in a variety of activities, and enjoy typical food, horse riding, photo safaris and nature watching. Another agency for visiting *estancias* in Misiones Province only is **Emitur**, T0782-20286, T222081 (Asunción only) or T9-7562 6780. See especially the **Ministry of Tourism** (SENATUR) web site, www.senatur.gov.py, as well as that of **Turismo Paraguay**, www.turismo.com.py, for a list of ranches that welcome tourists. All visits should be arranged at least one week in advance.

Tennis Academia de Tenis at Parque Seminario, 25 de Mayo y Kubicheck, T206379 to reserve a court. Price US$4.50 per hr daytime and US$5.50 per hr evening. Coaching available.

Tours

Many agencies offer day tours of the Circuito de Oro or Camino Franciscano (from US$50). Trips to local *estancias*, Encarnación and the former Jesuit Missions, Itaipú and Iguazú or the Chaco region are all offered as 1, 2 or 4-day tours. Prices from US$100. Most agencies will also provide personalized itineraries on request. City tours also available. For more information contact **Dirección General de Turismo** or the **Paraguayan Association of Travel Agencies and Tourism** (ASATUR), Juan O'Leary 650, p 1, T491728, www.asatur.org.py.
Alda Saguier, Yegros 941, p 2, T446492. For the Chaco and indigenous regions. English and German spoken.
Aries Travel, Paraguari 743 y Herrera, T450473, www.ariestravel.com.py.
Canadá Viajes, Rep de Colombia 1061, T211192, www.canadaviajes.com.py. Good Asunción and Chaco tours.
Crucero Paraguay, Pdte Franco 982, Edif Mocipar, p 3, T452328, www.crucero paraguay.info. Specialists in Chaco and Pantanal. 4-10 day cruises on the Río Paraguay, visits historical and ecological sites along the river, on-board entertainment, international menu, pool and cinema.
Inter Tours, Perú 436 y España, T211747, www.intertours.com.py. One of Paraguay's biggest full-service tour agencies. Tours to Chaco, Iguazú and Jesuit missions. Highly recommended.
Itra Travel, Venezuela 663 y España, T200020, www.itra.com.py. Also offer ecotourism, national park tours.
Menno Travel, Rep de Colombia 1042 entre Brasil y EEUU, T493504, mennotravel@gmx.net. German spoken.
Natura Express, Cruz del Defensor 137 y Mcal López, Barrio Villa Morra, T610353, www.natura-express.com. Adventure tourism, offering hiking, rappelling, kayaking, microlight flights, caving, riding and other activities, various packages.
Paraguay Natural/Barka Viajes, Gral Santos y 18 de Julio, T302027, www.paraguaynatural.com.py. Specialists in nature tourism throughout the country and Brazilian Pantanal.
Time Tours, 15 Agosto y Gral Díaz, T449737, also at O'Higgins 891 y Austria, Barrio Villa Mora, T611649, www.timetours.com.py. Fluent English, runs Camino Franciscano tours. Recommended.
Vips Tour, México 782 entre Fulgencio R Moreno y Herrera, T441199, www.vipstour.com.py. Asunción, estancia and Chaco tours.

Transport

Asunción *p15, map p16*

Air Silvio Pettirossi Airport, T645600. Several agencies have desks where you can book a taxi to your hotel, US$12-25. Bus 30 goes every 15 mins between the red bus stop outside the airport and Plaza de los Héroes, US$0.50, difficult with luggage. Minibus service from your hotel to airport run by **Tropical**, T424486, book in advance, US$8 (minimum 2 passengers, or pay for 2). The terminal has a tourist office (free city map and hotel information), bank (turn right as you leave customs – better rates in town), post office (0800-1800), handicraft shop, restaurant and several travel agencies who arrange hotel bookings and change money (very poor rates). Left luggage US$4.50 per day per item.

Bus *City buses*: Journeys within greater Asunción US$0.40. Buses can be busy at rush hours. Turnstiles are awkward for large backpacks. Keep your ticket for inspection until you leave bus.

Long-distance: The Terminal de Omnibus is south of the centre at República Argentina y Fernando de la Mora (T551740/1, www.mca.gov.py/webtermi.html). Local bus No 8 is the only direct one from Oliva, which goes via Cerro Corá and Av Brasil from the centre, and stops outside the terminal, US$0.40. From the terminal to the centre it goes via Av Estados Unidos, Luis A Herrera, Antequera and E Ayala; get off at Chile y Díaz. Other buses Nos 10, 25, 31, 38 and 80, follow very circuitous routes. Taxi to/from centre, recommended if you have luggage, US$3.65, journey time depends on the amount of traffic, about 45 mins. The terminal has a bus information desk, free city/country map, restaurant (quite good), café, *casa de cambio* (poor rates), post office, phone booths and shops. There are many touts for bus companies at the terminal. Allow yourself time to choose the company you want and don't be tricked into buying the wrong ticket. Better companies include: **Nuestra Señora de la Asunción**, T551725 or 289100, www.nsa.com.py, has booking office at main terminal and at Mcal Estigarribia y Antequera, off Plaza Uruguaya. **RYSA**, T444244, www.rysa.com.py. Bus company offices on the top floor are in 3 sections: short-distance, medium and long. Local departures, including for Yaguarón and Paraguarí, are boarded from the basement. Hotels nearby: turn left from front of terminal, 2 mins' walk. Bus times and fares within Paraguay are given under destinations.

To Argentina There is a road north from Asunción (passing the Jardín Botánico on Primer Presidente) to a concrete arch span bridge (Puente Remanso – US$1.25 toll, pedestrian walkway on upstream side, 20 mins to cross) which leads to the border at Puerto Falcón (about 40 km) and then to **Clorinda** in Argentina. The border is open 24 hrs; local services are run by **Empresa Falcón** to Puerto Falcón (US$1, every hour, last bus from Falcón to the centre of Asunción 1830; from Falcón to Clorinda costs US$0.55), but it is cheaper overall to book direct from Asunción to Argentina.

Note Buses don't wait for you to go through formalities: if you cannot process in time, wait for the same company's next bus and present ticket, or buy a new ticket.

Buses to **Buenos Aires** (18 hrs) daily, many companies, via Rosario and Santa Fe (average fare US$110-113 luxury, US$75 semi-cama). To **Resistencia** and **Corrientes**, 41 a day each, **El Pulqui** and **Crucero del Norte** (US$17-18) many drug searches on this road. To **Salta**, take a bus to **Resistencia**, then change to **Flecha** (www.flechabus.com) or **La Veloz del Norte** (www.lavelozcallcenter.com.ar).

To Brazil Many Paraguayan buses advertise that they go to destinations in Brazil, when, in fact you have to change buses and book again at the frontier. Services to **Campo Grande** and **Corumbá** via Pedro Juan Caballero and Ponta Porã do not stop for immigration formalities. Check all details carefully. **Nuestra Señora de la Asunción** and the Brazilian company **Pluma** (T551758, www.pluma.com.br) have direct services via Ciudad del Este to **Foz do Iguaçu** (Brazil), US$16.50-20, 5-7 hrs. Seat reservations recommended. To **Curitiba**, with **Pluma** and others, buses daily, 15½ hrs, US$47. To **Florianópolis** Catarinense (T551738, www.catarinense.net, Tue, Wed, Thu, Sat, Sun), 17 hrs, US$112 and **Pluma** (Mon, Wed, Fri), US$94. To **Porto Alegre**, Unileste (T442679), Tue, Thu. To **São Paulo**, Pluma and **Brújula**, 20 hrs, US$81. **Pluma** to **Rio de Janeiro**, US$120; Transcontinental (T557369) to **Brasília** 3 a week.

To Bolivia Via the Chaco, to Santa Cruz, Yacyretá, T551725, most reliable, Mon, Wed, Fri, and Sat at 2000. **Stel Turismo**, T558196, daily at 2000, **Pycazú**, Thu and Sat at 2100, but you cannot get on in Mariscal Estigarribia. All fares US$62. All buses normally travel via Mariscal Estigarribia, for Paraguayan immigration where foreigners must get an exit stamp; La Patria; Infante Rivarola at the border; Ibibobo, for Bolivian immigration; and Villamontes, to Santa Cruz. Advertised as 21 hrs, the trip can take 3 days if the bus breaks down. Some food provided but take your own, plus extra water just in case; also take toilet paper. The buses can be very crowded. In summer the route can be very hot and dusty, but in winter, it can be cold at night. Alternative route to Bolivia via Salta, Argentina (see above).

Unless specifically advertised, buses to Bolivia do not go through Filadelfia or the other Mennonite colonies, so take a local services from Asunción (see page 70). After visiting the Chaco, you can usually get on a Bolivia-bound bus in Mariscal Estigarribia, where the bus companies have agents (see page 69), but enquire in advance with their offices in Asunción.

To Uruguay EGA (Eligio Ayala 693, T492473, www.egakeguay.com) runs to **Montevideo** 3 times a week 20 hrs, US$115, as does **Brújula/Cynsa** (Pres Franco 995, T441720). The route is Encarnación, Posadas, Paso de los Libres, Uruguaiana, Bella Unión, Salto, Paysandú; the only customs formalities are at Bella Unión; passport checks here and at Encarnación.

River boat To escape the city take a short trip across the river to the **Mbiguá Club** to sunbathe and relax. Ask at Aduanas for information. A small launch leaves every 20 mins from the pier at the bottom of Montevideo to **Chaco-i**, a strip of land between the Ríos Paraguay and Pilcomayo, US$0.65 each way. The Argentine town of Clorinda is just the other side of the Pilcomayo. Ferry to **Puerto Pilcomayo** (Argentina) about every 30 mins, US$0.65 (Argentine immigration closed at weekends for tourists).

Boats for **Concepción** leave from the bottom of Montevideo. Offices for information/prices El Paraguayo Independiente 813 y Ayolas (not always staffed), T492829. Sailings weekly (Wed), 27-30 hrs, US$25 1st class, US$15 2nd, US$8 deck space (not recommended). Sleeping space is sometimes available. Take food, water, toilet paper, warm clothes, sleeping bag and mosquito repellent. If you want more luxury take a 5-star cruise on the **Crucero Paraguayo**, see **Tours**, above. Reservations also available through larger tour operators.

Taxi Minimum fare in Asunción: US$0.40, and US$0.10 per 100 m. Minimum fare is about 30-50% more at night. There are many taxi ranks throughout the city. Taxis can either be hailed or call **Radiotaxi** (recommended), T550116/311080.

Train A **tourist steam train** runs from Estación Botánico, outside the Jardín Botánico, to Areguá and Sapucaí, Sun 1030, return 1930, US$22 for foreigners, US$6 for Paraguayans, price includes soft drink, *empanadas* and on-board entertainment (actors presenting 19th-century scenes); 4-hr stop in Areguá for lunch and sightseeing. Highly recommended. You can buy tickets on the day or in advance from Estación San Roque, Ayala y Plaza Uruguaya. See page 53 for the locomotive workshops at Sapucaí. In 2011 track repairs temporarily closed this route. Visit www.ferrocarriles.com.py for the latest details.

Directory

Asunción *p15, map p16*
Airline offices Aerolíneas Argentinas, España 2220, T450577, www.aerolineas. com.ar. **AeroSur**, Senador Long 856 y España, T614743, www.aerosur.com. **Gol**, Paseo Carmelitas, España esq Malutin, T454777, www.voegol.com.br. **Iberia**, Senador Long 790 y Tte Vera, T214246, www.iberia.com/py. **LAN**, Juan de Salazar y Washington, T233487-9, www.lan.com. **Lufthansa**, N S de la Asunción 208, T447962, lhasu@cmm.com.py, admin and cargo only, no passenger flights, ticket information from travel agents. **TAM**, Oliva 761 y Ayolas, T645500, www.tam.com.py. **Banks** Be careful to count money received from street money changers (Palma and surrounding area – their rates are poor when banks and *cambios* are closed). See Money section in Planning your trip. Lots of ATMs, accepting credit and debit cards, give dollars and guaraníes. **HSBC**, Palma y O'Leary, T419 7000, (as well as several other branches in Greater Asunción). Accepts Visa. **Citibank**, CitiCenter, Av Mcal López 3794 y Cruz del Chaco, T620200. Will change Citibank TCs into US$ cash, and gives US$ cash on MasterCard credit card. **ABN AMRO**, Estrella 443 y Alberdi (main office), T419000, clientes@py.abnamro.com; also at Av San Martín 763 y Lillo, T611513; Eusebio Ayala y Mayor Bullo, T225854; and Shopping Mariscal López, T608977, accepts several cards. **Interbanco**, Oliva 349 y Chile, T494992, ATM at Shopping Del Sol, accepts Visa. **Amex**, at Inter-Express, Yegros 690, T490111, iexpress@interexpress.com.py. To change TCs other than American Express you must go to Banco Santander, Banespa, Independencia Nacional y Moreno, good rates, proof of purchase required. Many **casas de cambio** on Palma, Estrella and nearby streets (open Mon-Fri 0730-1200, 1500-1830, Sat 0730-1200). All rates are better than at frontiers. They change dollars, euros, Brazilian reais, Argentine pesos and a few will accept sterling notes or Bolivianos. Some **casas de cambio** change only dollar-denominated TCs. **Cambios Chaco**, on Palma and at Shopping Mscal López. **Maxi Cambio**, in Shopping del Sol. Good rates for dollars cash. **Parapiti Cambios/ Financiera Guaraní**, Palma 449, T490032, change TCs (small fee). Mon-Fri 0830-1730, Sat 0830-1200. **Sudamérica Express**, 14 de Mayo 340, T445305, www.tupi.com.py, 3 other locations in capital. Decent rates for TCs. **Cambios Yguazú**, 15 de Agosto 451, T448018, no commission. **Car hire** Fast Rent a Car, Prof Chávez 1276 y Santa Rosa, T605462, www.fastrentacar.com.py. Good, helpful. Also other companies at the airport. See Planning your trip for international rental agencies. **Cultural centres** Alianza Francesa, Mcal Estigarribia 1039 y Estados Unidos, T210503, www.alianzafrancesa. edu.py. Snack bar. **Centro Cultural Paraguayo Americano**, España 352 entre Brasil y Estados Unidos, T224831, www.ccpa.edu.py. Has a good library (Mon-Fri 0900-2000, Sat 0900-1200, also has snack bar). **Centro Paraguayo-Japonés**, Av Julio Corea y Domingo, T607276, www.centro paraguayojapones.blogspot.com. Has a good theatre. **Instituto Cultural Paraguayo Alemán**, Juan de Salazar 310 y Artigas,

T226242, www.icpa-gz.org.py. Recommended. All institutes have special events, films, etc.
Embassies and consulates Argentina, España y Perú, T212320, www.embajada-argentina.org.py. Visas issued at Edif Banco Nacional de Argentina, Palma 319, p1, T442151, open 0800-1300, 1500-1800, 2-hr service, photo needed (if you require a multiple entry visa, get it in your country of residence). Also consulates in Ciudad del Este and Encarnación. **Australia**, Hon Consul, Prócer Argüello 208 entre Mcal López y Bollani, T608740. **Austrian Consulate**, Aviadores del Chaco 1690, T613316, consuladoaustria@rolitrans.com.py. Mon-Fri 0730-1100. **Belgian** Hon Consul, Daniel Ceuppens, Ruta 2, Km 17, Capiatá, T0228-633326. Mon-Fri 1000-1400. **Bolivia**, Eligio Ayala 2002, T210676. Mon-Fri 0900-1300. **Brazil**, Coronel Irrazabal y Eligio Ayala, T248400, www.embajada brasil.org.py, open 0800-1400, Mon-Fri, US$25 for visa. **Canadian Consulate**, Prof Ramírez 3 y Juan de Salazar, T227207. Mon-Fri 0800-1300 (nearest embassy Buenos Aires). **Danish Consulate**, N S de la Asunción 76, T490617, Mon-Fri 0730-1130, 1500-1830. **Dutch Consulate**, Artigas 4145, T283665, connederland@cmp.com.py, Mon-Fri 0900-1600. **Finland**, Hon Consul, Elias Ayala 295 y Yasy, T291175 (the nearest embassy is in Brasilia). **France**, España 893 y Padre Pucheu, T212449, www.ambafrance-py.org, Mon-Fri 0800-1200. **Germany**, Av Venezuela 241, T214009, www.asuncion.diplo.de. 0800-1100 Mon-Fri. **Israel**, De la Residentas 685 y Boquerón, T221486, consulis@gmail.com. **Italy**, Quesada 5871 y Bélgica, T615620, www.ambassunzione.esteri.it. **Japan**, Av Mcal López 2364, T604616. Mon-Fri 0800-1200, 1500-1730. **New Zealand**, Hon Consul, Eduardo Gustale, O'Leary 795 esq Humaitá, T496498, egustale@rieder.net.py. **Spain**, Yegros 437, p 5 y 6, T490686/7, embesppy@correo.mae.es. Mon-Fri 0830-1300. **Sweden**, Hon Consul, Artigas 1945, T219003, erika.domann@citsa.com.py. Mon-Fri 0730-1200, 1330-1730. **Switzerland**, O'Leary 409, p 4, of 423, T490848. 0800-1230 Mon-Fri. **UK**, Hon Consul, Eulogio Estigarribia 4846 y Monseñor Bogarin, T210405, guillermo.peroni@pstbn.com.py, Mon-Fri 0800-1300 and 1500-1900, nearest Embassy in Buenos Aires. **Uruguay**, Guido Boggiani 5832 y Alas Paraguayas, p 3, T664244, conurupar@telesurf.com.py. Visas processed immediately if exit ticket from Uruguay, overland travel to Uruguay and onward country visas can be shown. Mon-Fri 0700-1730. **US Embassy and Consulate**, Av Mcal López 1776, T213715, http://paraguay.usembassy.gov. Mon-Fri 0730-1730.
Immigration Caballero y Eligio Ayala, T446066, www.migraciones.gov.py.
Internet Lots of internet cafés in and around Asunción. The average price is US$0.75-1 per hr. **Cyber Shop**, Estrella 480 and Alberdi y 14 de Mayo, T446290, helpful. **Interspace Internet**, 25 de Mayo y Antequera, T119190. **Patio de Luz Internet Café**, Azara 248, T449741. Also bar, restaurant, occasional live music. Internet near food hall in Shopping Villa Morra. **Unicom**, Papa Juan XXIII y Gómez (behind Shopping del Sol), T/F610902. Very helpful, fax and DVD rental.
Language schools Idipar (Idiomas en Paraguay), Manduvirá 963, T447896, www.idipar.edu.py. Offers courses in Spanish or Guaraní. Private or group lessons available, also offers accommodation with local families and volunteer opportunities. 60 hrs per week from US$340 in groups, US$21 per hr for private lessons. Good standard.
Medical services Private hospitals: **Bautista**, Av Argentina y Cervera, T600171/4. **Sanatorio San Roque**, Eligio Ayala y Pa'í Pérez, T212499/ 228700, 24 hrs. Public hospital: **Emergencias Médicas**, Brasil y FR Moreno, T204800/204715. Pharmacies: There are numerous pharmacies throughout Asunción, many offering 24-hr service.

Farmacia Vicente Scavone, Palma y 15 de Agosto, T490396. **Farmacia Catedral Centro**, Palma e Independencia Nacional, Plaza de los Héroes. Both reliable. **Post offices** Alberdi, between Benjamín Constant y El Paraguayo Independiente, T498112. Mon-Fri 0700-2000, Sat 0700-1200. **Poste Restante** (ask at the Casillas section) charges about US$0.50 per item, but you may have to insist they double-check if you are expecting letters (poste restante closes 1100). Postcards for sale, but better ones in nearby bookshops. Packages under 2 kg should be handed in at the small packages window, over 2 kg at the 'Encomiendas' office in the same building, but on other end at corner of Alberdi and Benjamín Constant. A faster and more reliable way to send parcels is by EMS, the post office courier service from the same office. Customs inspection of open parcel required. Register all important mail. There are sub-offices at Shopping del Sol, Shopping Villa Morra and in certain suburbs, but mail takes longer to arrive from these offices. **Telephones** Phone booths can be found on almost every block of central Asunción for international calls and fax, 24 hrs.

Región Oriental: East of Asunción

To the east of the Río Paraguay lie the most fertile lands and the most populated region of the country. Of the vast rainforests that once covered it, only a few isolated patches have not been converted to farmland. Ruta 2 and Ruta 7 head east towards the border with Brazil, taking the traveller through tranquil villages known for their arts and crafts, German colonies and small towns associated with the country's bloody past. In contrast to the quiet of the countryside, Ciudad del Este is a crossroads for all manner of merchandise, much of it illegal, and the world's largest stolen car market, while the giant Itaipú dam has irreversibly changed the landscape. Just over the border are the Iguazú Falls.

Itauguá → *Phone code: 0294. Population: 94,896.*
At Km 30, founded in 1728, Itauguá, now Paraguay's fastest-growing city, is where the famous *ñandutí*, or spiderweb lace, is made. There are more than 200 different designs. Prices are lower than in Asunción and the quality is better; there are many makers, but try Taller Artesanal (Km 29), Mutual Tejedoras (Km 28), or Casa Miryam (Km 30, T20372). Almost all of the best *talleres* are located directly off of the highway and can be accessed by bus. To watch the lace being made, ask around. The old town lies two blocks from the main highway. Worth seeing are the **market** ⓘ *0800-1130, 1500-1800, closed Sun*, the church and the **Museo de Historia Indígena** ⓘ *Km 25, daily 0800-1130, 1500-1800, US$0.60*, a beautiful collection of carvings of Guaraní mythological creatures, and the **Museo Parroquial San Rafael** ⓘ *daily 0800-1130, 1500-1800*, with a display of indigenous art and Franciscan artefacts. There is a four-day **Festival de Ñandutí** in early July, including processions and the crowning of Señorita Ñandutí. Many of Paraguay's best traditional musicians perform during the festival. Itauguá is also the birthplace of Juan Crisóstomo Centurión, the only Paraguayan military leader to win a battle in the War of the Triple Alliance and an architect of the country's rebirth. The best guide for information about town is online: http://itauguacity.110mb.com/

Areguá → *Phone code: 0291. Population: 67,487.*
At **Capiatá** (Ruta 2, Km 20, fine colonial church), a left turn goes to **Areguá**. Founded in 1541 this is a pretty colonial village, 28 km southeast of Asunción on the slopes above **Lago Ypacaraí**. Formerly the summer capital of the country's elite, from its attractive church at the highest point in town there is one of the best views of the lake and surroundings. It has an interesting ceramics cooperative, a museum, arts and crafts exhibition and a convent. There is a good German-run restaurant in the centre of the village. From here boat trips run across the lake at weekends to San Bernadino and the tourist steam train (when operating) comes here each Sunday from Asunción on its way to Sapucaí.

San Bernardino and Lago Ypacaraí → *Phone code: 0512. Population, 9491.*

At Km 40 on Ruta 2 a branch road, 8 km long, leads off to **San Bernardino**, originally a German colony, known locally as 'Samber', on the east bank of Lago Ypacaraí. The lake, 24 km by 5 km, has facilities for swimming and watersports and sandy beaches (ask locally about pollution levels in the water). There are frequent cruises from the pier during the tourist season. This is now the main vacation spot for Asunción from December to February, which means that it is lively and crowded at weekends in the summer, with concerts, pubs and nightclubs, but as a result it is commercialized. During the week and off season it is a tranquil resort town, with lakeside tourism clearly the main draw. Boats can be hired and there is good walking in the neighbourhood, for example from San Bernardino to **Altos**, which has one of the most spectacular views of the lake, wooded hills and valleys (round trip three hours). Shortly after the turn off from the main road towards San Bernardino is a sign to **La Gruta**; turn right here to a secluded park (Ypacaraí). There are grottos with still water and overhanging cliffs. No buses run after 2000 and taxis are expensive. Tourist information is in the centre of town between General Morinigo and Emilio Hassler.

Caacupé → *Phone code: 0511. Population: 42,127. www.caacupe.com.py*

At Km 54 on Ruta 2, this is a popular resort and religious centre on the Azcurra escarpment. The centre is dominated by the modern Basilica of Our Lady of the Miracles, with a copper roof, stained glass and polychrome stone esplanade, consecrated by Pope John Paul II in 1988 (US$0.25 to climb the tower). There is an ATM on the plaza between the supermarket and Hotel El Mirador.

Thousands of people from Paraguay, Brazil and Argentina flock to the shrine, especially for the **Fiesta de la Inmaculada Concepción** on 8 December. Besides fireworks and candlelit processions, pilgrims watch the agile gyrations of Paraguayan bottle-dancers; they weave in intricate measures whilst balancing bottles pyramided on their heads. The top bottle carries a spray of flowers and the more expert dancers never let drop a single petal.

Tobati, a town north of Caacupé, specializes in woodwork. The *villa artesenal* is a short walk from the bus stop outside the house of the late **Zenon Páez**, a world famous sculptor. There are some amazing rock formations on the way to Tobati. To get there, take a bus from the corner below the park on the main Asunción road in Caacupé.

Piribebuy → *Phone code: 0515. Population: 21,800.*

Beyond Caacupé, at Km 64, a paved road runs 13 km southeast to the town of Piribebuy, founded in 1640 and noted for its strong local drink, *caña*. In the central plaza is the church (1640), with fine sculptures, high altar and pulpit. The town was the site of a major battle in the War of the Triple Alliance (1869), commemorated by the **Museo Histórico Pedro Juan Caballero** ⓘ *free*. Buses from Asunción by Transportes Piribebuy. Near the town are the attractive falls of Pirareta. The road continues via Chololó, 13 km south, and reaches Ruta 1 at Paraguarí, 28 km from Piribebuy (see page 53). Between Pirbebuy and Paraguarí is an outdoor and adventure centre, **Eco-reserva Mbatoví** ⓘ *US$3.50, T9-7129 9250, for reservations and information visit www.mbatovi.com.py*, with a visitor centre. It includes an outdoor pursuits course ⓘ *US$36.75*, and a two-hour guided walk ⓘ *US$15*, taking in early settlements, local folklore and beautiful scenery.

Vapor Cué National Park

A turn-off from Eusebio Ayala (Km 72) goes 23 km to **Caraguatay**, 5 km from which is the Vapor Cué National Park, where boats from the War of the Triple Alliance are preserved. Although officially a national park, it is more of an open-air museum. Next to the (indoor) museum is a pleasant hotel, **Hotel Nacional de Vapor Cué** (**$**, T0517-222395). Frequent buses run from Asunción to Caraguatay.

North from Coronel Oviedo

Coronel Oviedo (*Phone code 0521; population: 58,120*), at the junction of west-east highway Ruta 2 and the major north-south Ruta 8, is an important route centre, although hardly worth a stop. Buses drop passengers for connections at the junction (El Cruce). Ruta 8 runs north to **Mbutuy**, continuing as Ruta 3 to Yby Yaú, where it meets Ruta 5 (Concepción-Pedro Juan Caballero). At Mbutuy (Km 56, parador, restaurant, petrol station) Ruta 10 branches off northeast to the Brazilian frontier at **Salto del Guaíra** (*Phone code: 046*), named after the waterfalls now under the Itaipú lake. There is a 900-ha wildlife reserve, Refugio Biológico Mbaracayú (www.itaipubinacional.gov.py/node/412). Salto del Guaíra, a free port, can also be reached by a paved road which runs north from Hernandarias, via Itaquyry to meet Ruta 10 at Cruce Carambey.

Mbaracayú Forest Reserve ⓘ *To visit you must book and pay in advance, and sign a disclaimer at the Moisés Bertoni Foundation in Asunción (see National Parks, page 7 for address); entry US$7.50, lodging US$16.85 pp, camping US$12.50 per tent, take your own food, cook available US$10 per day plus US$3 per day for gas, transport US$0.35 per km. No walk-ins allowed. You must hire a guide for US$23.50 per day, without you will only be allowed to camp near the entrance. There is public transport to Villa Ygatimi from where they pick you up, 20 km to the park. Pay ahead for transport you will require within the park. Buses from Asunción to Curuguaty: La Coruguateña and Santa Ana, 0900 and 1430, 6 hrs, US$5.80. From Curuguaty to Ygatimi local buses take 1 hr.* Not to be confused with the nearby Refugio Biológico Mbaracayú mentioned above, this federally protected reserve covers more than 66,000 ha of Paraguay's rapidly disappearing Interior Atlantic forest. It is the largest area representative of this ecosystem in good conservation status in Paraguay. It contains 48% of all mammal species and 63% of all bird species (over 400) found in eastern Paraguay. There are trails, waterfalls and spectacular view points. There are also two indigenous communities, the Aché and Guaraní. There is a visitor centre and small museum at Villa Ygatimi.

At Santa Rosa, 143 km north of Mbutuy, there is petrol, *pensión* and restaurants. A dirt road runs southwest for 27 km to **Nueva Germania** founded in 1866 by Bernhard Förster and Elisabeth Nietzsche (the philosopher's sister) to establish a pure Aryan colony. This road goes on to San Pedro and Puerto Antequera on the Río Paraguay (88 km). A further 23 km north of Santa Rosa, a dirt road runs northeast through jungle to the interesting **Capitán Badó** (120 km), which forms the frontier with Brazil. From here a road follows the frontier north to Pedro Juan Caballero (100 km). About 50 km north of the turn off to Capitán Badó is Yby Yaú, see page 61.

Villarrica → *Phone code: 0541. Population: 56,385.*

Villarrica, 42 km south of Coronel Oviedo, is delightfully set on a hill rich with orange trees. A very pleasant, friendly place, it has a fine cathedral, built in traditional style with veranda, and various pleasant parks. The museum (closed weekends) behind the church has a foreign coin collection; please contribute. Products of the region are tobacco, cotton, sugar, yerba mate, hides, meat and wine produced by German settlers. There is a large student population.

There are several German colonies near Villarrica. Some 7 km north is an unsigned turn off to the east, then 20 km to tiny **Colonia Independencia**, which has some beautiful beaches on the river (popular in summer). German-speaking travellers can also visit the German cooperative farms (these are not Mennonite communities, but rather German settlements established in the early 20th century). A great mate and wine producing area and, at harvest time, there is a wine festival. They also have beer festival in October.

East from Coronel Oviedo

The paved Ruta 7 runs 195 km through farmed areas and woods and across the Caaguazú hills. From here it continues to the spectacular 500-m single span 'Friendship Bridge' across the Paraná (to Brazil) at Ciudad del Este.

Ciudad del Este → *Phone code: 061.*
Population: 320,782.

Originally founded as Ciudad Presidente Stroessner in 1957, this was the fastest growing city in the country until the completion of the Itaipú hydroelectric project, for which it is the centre of operations. Ciudad del Este has been described as the biggest shopping centre in Latin America, attracting Brazilian and Argentine visitors who find bargain prices for electrical goods, watches and perfumes. However, it is a counterfeiter's paradise and can be quite dangerous. Check everything properly before making a purchase and ensure that shops pack what you actually bought. The main shopping street is Avenida San Blas, lined with shopping malls and market stalls, selling a huge variety of goods, both original and imitations – usually the latter. Almost any vehicle advertised for sale, should you be tempted, was stolen in Brazil or Bolivia. Many jewels and stones are also counterfeit; be especially careful with touts advertising amethysts or emeralds. Watch the exchange rates if you're a short-term visitor. Parts are of the city are dirty and frantic during business hours, but away from the shopping arcades people are

Ciudad del Este

Sleeping
Austria 1
California 2
Caribe 3
Convair 4
Executive 5
Munich 7
New Cosmos Apart-Hotel 8
Panorama Inn 9
Tía Nancy 11

friendly and more relaxed. The leather market is well worth a visit, be sure to bargain. **Tourist office** ⓘ *Coronel Rafael Franco entre Pampliega y Curupayty, Edificio Líbano p 1 of 104, T866264; municipal website: www.mcde.gov.py.*

Around Ciudad del Este The **Monday falls** ⓘ *0700-1700, US$0.45, taxi US$20 return*, where the Río Monday drops into the Paraná gorge, are worth seeing. Nearby is the popular beach resort and biological refuge called **Tatí Yupí** ⓘ *www.itaipu.gov.py*. Two other biological reserves border the Itaipú dam, **Itabó** and, further north, **Limoy**. Take the unpaved road north from Ciudad del Este towards Salto del Guaíra. Itabó is at the first turn off to Dorila, and Limoy the turnoff at Colonia San Lorenzo.

Border with Brazil

The border crossing over the Friendship Bridge to Foz do Iguaçu is very informal, but is jammed with vehicles and pedestrians all day long. No passport stamps are required to visit Ciudad del Este for the day. Motorcycle taxis (helmet provided, hang on tight) are a good option if you have no luggage. Otherwise, to enter Paraguay here, hire a taxi and go very early in the morning, or take your gear to the Paraguayan bus terminal (left luggage facilities, keep ticket) by city bus, then shuttle back and forth on foot to get passport stamped; it is a long and tiring process. (Make sure you get a Paraguayan entry stamp; without it you will be fined. If you do get fined, get a receipt.) Immigration formalities for Paraguay and Brazil are dealt with on opposite sides of the bridge. There is a friendly tourist office in the customs building on the Paraguayan side. Remember to adjust your watch to local time (Brazil is one hour ahead). The **Brazilian consulate** ⓘ *Ciudad del Este, Pampliega 205 esq Pa'í Pérez, T061-500984, consulado@consbrascde.org.py, Mon-Fri 0700*, issues visas. The **Argentine Consulate** ⓘ *Av Boquerón y Adrián Jara, Edificio China p 7, T061-500945, ccest@mrecic.gov.ar.*

Itaipú and around

ⓘ *www.itaipu.gov.py, Mon-Fri 0730-1200, 1330-1700, Sat, Sun and holidays 0800-1100. Bus tours Mon-Fri 0800, 0930, 1400, 1500, Sat 0800, 0930, 1030, 1400, 1500 (morning only Sun and holidays). Free tours of the project with film show (several languages). Take passport. Buses going to Hernandarias will drop you at the visitor centre.*

The Itaipú project (a huge hydroelectric project covering an area of 1350 sq km and still subject to controversy among environmental groups) is close to Ciudad del Este, and well worth a visit.

On the way to Itaipú is **Flora y Fauna Itaipú Binacional** ⓘ *www.itaipu.gov.br, 0730-1130, 1400-1700*, a zoo and museum containing native animals and plants; it is about 2 km from the visitor's centre on the road back to Ciudad del Este. At the Centro Ambiental de Itaipú is the **Museo de la Tierra Guaraní** ⓘ *T061-599 8040, Tue-Sat 0800-1130, 1430-1700 (Mon afternoon only), Sun 0800-1130*, which offers a view of the science and culture of the Guaraníes via natural history displays and interactive screens.

Hernandarias, just north of Ciudad del Este grew rapidly with the building of Itaipú. A paved road runs north to Cruce Carambey, where it meets Ruta 10 (see above, page 33). From Hernandarias, boat trips on Lago Itaipú go to Puerto Guaraní where there is a museum.

East of Asunción listings

For Sleeping and Eating price codes and other relevant information, see, pages 9-10.

Sleeping

San Bernardino *p32*
There are plenty of hotels other than those listed, many with good restaurants (eg **de Sol** and **Los Alpes**, US$3.50 for buffet lunch and use of pool).

$$$$ Sol de San Ber, Rosa Mendola y Tte Weiler, T233138, pueblo@telesurf.com.py. New, super luxury.

$$$ Del Lago, Tte Weiler 401 y Mcal López, near lake in town, T232201, www.hoteldel lago.org. With breakfast, attractive 1888 building recently renovated as a museum, upgraded, a/c, fan, safe, Wi-Fi, regional decor, restaurant, bar and grill, pool, lovely gardens.

$$ Los Alpes, Ruta General Morínigo Km 46.5, 3 km from town, T232083, www.hotellos alpes.com.py. A/c, cable TV, Wi-Fi, internet, lovely gardens, 2 pools, excellent self-service restaurant, children's playground, beach 1 km away, frequent buses to centre.

$$ San Bernardino Pueblo, C 8 entre C 5 y Mbocayá, T232195, pueblohotel@hotmail. com. Swimming pool, a/c, by the lake. Weekend packages, 2 nights for US$74 pp.

Camping Brisas del Mediterraneo, Ruta Kennedy a 2000 m from Copaco, T232459, www.campingparaguay.org. With beach, games.

Caacupé *p32*
Cheaper than Lago Ypacaraí. Prices increase during the Fiesta de la Inmaculada Concepción.

$ El Mirador, T242652, on plaza. With bath.
$ Katy María, Eligio Ayala y Dr Pino, T242860, beside Basílica. Well-kept, welcoming.
$ Virgen Serrana, plaza, T242366. Cheaper with fan.

Camping West of Tobati is **Atyrá** (15 km from Caacupé), 2 camp grounds: **Chorro Carumbey** and **Balneario Atyrá**.

Tourism farm
$$$ Estancia Aventura, Km 61.5, Ruta 2, T9-8144 1804, www.estancia-aventura.com. 225 acres of countryside, 7-day packages. Owner speaks German, English, Spanish. Good, horse riding, tennis, swimming, tours, can arrange airport pickup from Asunción. Expensive but worth it.

Piribebuy *p32*
$$ pp La Quinta, 10 km from Piribebuy, 19 km from Paraguarí, 82.5 km from Asunción (take bus to Piribebuy then bus to Chololó, bus passes in front of hotel), T971-117444, www.laquinta. com.py. Price based on 4 sharing in cabins, also suites, also open for day visits, own stream and is close to falls at Piraretá and Chololó.

$ Viejo Rincón, Maestro Fermín López esq Tte Horacio Gini, T0515-212251. Reasonable.

Coronel Oviedo and around: Salto del Guaíra *p33*
$ Peralta, Av Paraguay y Capitán Capii Pery, T242235. Pleasant, with breakfast and bath, some rooms without.

Villarrica *p33*
$$$ Villarrica Palace Hotel, Ruta 8 Blas Garay, turn right on road entering Villarrica, T42832, www.sosahoteles.com. Large modern hotel, restaurant, parking, pool, sauna.

$$ Ybytyruzú, C A López y Dr Bottrell, T42390. Best in town, breakfast, more with a/c, restaurant.

$ Central Comuneros y Pa'i Anasagasti, by Plaza Ybaroty at entrance to town. With bath, a/c, electric shower, family run.

$ Guairá, Mcal López y Talavera, T42369. With bath and a/c, cheaper with fan, friendly.

German colonies near Villarica: Colonia Independencia *p34*
$ Hotel Tilinski, out of town, T0548-265240. Peaceful, German spoken, swimming pool (filled with river water), meals for residents.
Camping There is camping nearby at Melgarejo.

East from Coronel Oviedo *p34*
$$ pp Estancia Golondrina, José Domingo Ocampo, Km 235, T0527-20122 or 9-7141 7440, www.ges-py.com, or Asunción office T021-201521 (weekdays only), or through APATUR (see Rural tourism, page 24). Take the unpaved road to the right, 17 km to the ranch. A good place for combining rural and ecotourism. The ranch has extensive agricultural land as well as 12,000 ha of protected virgin forest (Reserva Ypetí) and abundant wildlife. There are trails for walking or horse riding, boat trips on the river, picturesque accommodation (a/c, private bathroom, very comfortable) overlooking the river. Price includes all meals and transportation from the main road.

Ciudad del Este *p34, map p34*
$$$ Convair, Adrián Jara y Pioneros del Este, T508555, www.hotelconvair.com. In shopping district, newly remodelled. A/c, comfortable, breakfast included. Restaurant good, pasta festival on Thu, pool. Bus to Foz do Iguaçu stop across the road.
$$ California, C A López 180, T500378, www.hotelcalifornia.com.py. Including breakfast, TV, a/c, several blocks from commercial area, large, modern with swimming pool, lit clay tennis court, attractive gardens, restaurant, good local surubi fish.
$$ Panorama Inn Pampliega y Eusebio Alaya, T500110, www.hotelpanoramainn.com.py. Modern, corporate atmosphere, breakfast.

$ Austria (also known as Viena), E R Fernández 165, T504213, www.hotelaustria restaurante.com. Above restaurant, good breakfast, a/c, Austrian family, good views from upper floors. Warmly recommended.
$ Caribe, Miranda y Fernández, opposite Hotel Austria, T512450. A/c, hot water, nice, garden, helpful owner. Recommended.
$ Munich, Fernández y Miranda, T500347. With breakfast, a/c, garage. Recommended.
$ New Cosmos Apart-Hotel, Edif Cosmopolitan 1, Pa'iPa'iérez y Pampliega, T511030. Apartment style with kitchenette and living room.
$ Tía Nancy, Arturo Garcete y Cruz del Chaco, by terminal, T502974. With electric shower, clean and convenient for bus station.

Eating

Villarrica *p33*
Many eating places on CA López and General Díaz. Good restaurants are **La Tranquera** (good value, more expensive at weekends), **Asunción**, **Casa Vieja** and **La Cocina de Mamá**. At night on the plaza with the Municipalidad stands sell tasty, cheap steaks. Good nightclubs are **Monasterio** (the most popular) and **La Tirana**, great atmosphere.

German colonies near Villarica: Colonia Independencia *p34*
Che Valle Mi, Correo Melgarejo. Recommended.
Ulli y Klaus, restaurant next door. Recommended.

Ciudad del Este *p34, map p34*
Cheaper restaurants along García and the market. Fast food chains in centre.
Mi Ranchero, Adrián Jara. Good food and prices. **New Tokyo**, Arco Iris supermarket, Bernardino Caballero. Good, authentic Japanese.
Osaka, Adrián Jara. Good, authentic Japanese.
Patussi Grill, Monseñor Francisco Cedzich casi Av Alejo García. Good churrasquería.

Transport

Itauguá *p31*
Bus Frequent from **Asunción**, 1 hr, US$0.50.

Areguá *p31*
Bus From **Asunción**, Transportes Ypacaraínse, every 30 mins, but do not leave from the terminal; alternatively take local bus to Capiatá and change.

San Bernardino *p32*
Bus From **Asunción**, 3 companies: Altos, Loma Grande and Ciudad de San Bernadino, every 10 mins, 45 km, 1-2 hrs, US$0.60.

Caacupé *p32*
Bus From **Asunción**, US$0.60, get off at Basilica (closer to centre) rather than Caacupé station.

Coronel Oviedo and around: Salto del Guaíra *p33*
Bus To **Asunción**, US$11.75, 5 daily; to **Ciudad del Este**, US$8. **To Brazil** Regular launches cross the lake to Guaíra, 20 mins, US$1.30. Also hourly bus service, 30 mins, US$1.30. Buses run north of the lake to Mondo Novo, where they connect with Brazilian services. Brazilian Consulate is at Destacamento de Caballería y Defensores del Chaco, T24-2305.

Villarrica *p33*
Bus To **Coronel Oviedo**, US$1.65. To **Asunción**, frequent, US$3.30, 3½ hrs (Empresa Guaireña). Also direct service to **Ciudad del Este**, 4 daily, US$3.65, 4 hrs.

German colonies near Villarrica: Colonia Independencia *p34*
Bus Direct to **Asunción**, 3 daily (US$1.65, 4 hrs), as well as to **Villarrica**.

Ciudad del Este *p34, map p34*
Air Full jet airport, Aeropuerto Guaraní. To **Asunción**, TAM daily en route from São Paulo. **TAM**, Curupayty 195 y Eusebio Alaya, T506030-35.

Bus Terminal is on the southern outskirts, T510421 (No 4 bus from centre, US$0.50, taxi US$3, recommended). Many buses to and from **Asunción**, US$16 rápido, 4½ hrs, at night only; US$8-10 común, 5 hrs. **Nuestra Señora** recommended (they also have an office in Shopping Mirage, Pampliega y Adrián Jara), **Rysa** (T501201) and others. To **Villarrica**, 10 a day, last 1620, 4 hrs, US$3 (**Guaireña**). To **Pedro Juan Caballero**, 7 hrs, overnight US$8.50. To **Concepción**, **García**, 11 hrs, 2 per day. To **Encarnación** (for Posadas and Argentina), paved road, frequent, 4 hrs, US$5.50 (this is cheaper than via Foz do Iguaçu).

Border with Brazil *p35*
Bus The international bus goes from outside the Ciudad del Este terminal to the Rodoviária in Foz. There are also local buses from the terminal and along Av Adrián Jara, every 15 mins, 0600-2000, US$0.60, which go to the city terminal (*terminal urbana*) in Foz. Most buses will not wait at immigration, so disembark to get your exit stamp, walk across the bridge (10 mins) and obtain your entry stamp; keep your ticket and continue to Foz on the next bus free. Paraguayan taxis cross freely to Brazil (US$21-23.50), but it is cheaper and easier to walk across the bridge and then take a taxi, bargain hard. You can pay in either currency (and often in Argentine pesos). Obtain all necessary exit and entry stamps.
To Argentina Direct buses to **Puerto Iguazú**, leave frequently from outside the terminal, US$1. If continuing into Argentina, you need to get Argentine and Paraguayan

stamps (not Brazilian), but bus usually does not stop, so ask driver if he will. Also check what stamps you need, if any, if making a day visit to Puerto Iguazú.

Itaipu and around: Hernandarias *p35*
Bus Frequent from **Ciudad del Este**, US$0.50.

Directory

Ciudad del Este *p34, map p34*
Banks Local banks (open Mon-Fri 0730-1100). **Citibank**, Adrián Jara y Curupayty. ATM, changes TCs, 0830-1200. **Amex**, Curupayty casi Adrián Jara, T502259. Dollars and guaraníes can be changed into reais in town. Several *casas de cambio*: **Cambio Guaraní**, Av Monseñor Rodríguez, changes TCs for US$0.75, branch on Friendship Bridge has good rates for many currencies including dollars and reais, but there is a long wait. **Cambios Alberdi**, Adrián Jara by Hotel Puerta del Sol, good rates. *Casa de cambio* rates are better than street rates. Money changers (not recommended) operate at the bus terminal but not at the Brazilian end of the Friendship Bridge. **Internet** Setik Technology, Av Tte Morales y 29 de Setiembre, T509009. **Cyber Café**, Shopping Mirage, Pampliega y Adrián Jara. **Telephones** Copaco, Alejo García y Pa'í Pérez, near centre on road to bus terminal, for international calls.

Iguazú Falls (Foz do Iguaçu)

The mighty Iguazú Falls are the most overwhelmingly magnificent in all of South America. So impressive are they that Eleanor Roosevelt remarked "poor Niagara" on witnessing them (they are four times wider). Viewed from below, the tumbling water is majestically beautiful in its setting of begonias, orchids, ferns and palms. Toucans, flocks of parrots and cacique birds and great dusky swifts dodge in and out along with myriad butterflies (there are at least 500 different species). Above the impact of the water, upon basalt rock, hovers a perpetual 30-m high cloud of mist in which the sun creates blazing rainbows.

Ins and outs

Information Entry is US$24.55, payable in pesos only. Argentines, Mercosur and Misiones inhabitants pay less. Entry next day is half price with same ticket, which you must get stamped at the end of the first day. Open daily 0800-1800. Visitor Centre includes information and photographs of the flora and fauna, as well as books for sale. There are places to eat, toilets, shops and a locutorio in the park. In the rainy season, when water levels are high, waterproof coats or swimming costumes are advisable for some of the lower catwalks and for boat trips. Cameras should be carried in a plastic bag. **Tourist offices** ⓘ *Aguirre 311, Puerto Iguazú, T420800,* and **Municipal office** ⓘ *Av Victoria Aguirre y Balbino Brañas, T422938, 0900-2200, www.iguazuturismo.gov.ar, also www.camara turismoiguazu.org.ar and www.iguazuargentina.com.* National park office: ⓘ *Victoria Aguirre 66, T420722, iguazu@apn.gov.ar.*

The falls, on the Argentina-Brazil border, are 19 km upstream from the confluence of the Río Iguazú with the Río Alto Paraná. The Río Iguazú (I is Guaraní for water and guazú is Guaraní for big), which rises in the Brazilian hills near Curitiba, receives the waters of some 30 rivers as it crosses the plateau. Above the main falls, the river, sown with wooded islets, opens out to a width of 4 km. There are rapids for 3.5 km above the 74 m precipice over which the water plunges in 275 falls over a frontage of 2470 m, at a rate of 1750 cu m a second (rising to 12,750 cu m in the rainy season).

Around the falls → *In Oct-Mar (daylight saving dates change each year) Brazil is 1 hr ahead.*
On both sides of the falls there are National Parks. Transport between the two parks is via the Ponte Tancredo Neves as there is no crossing at the falls themselves. The Brazilian park offers a superb panoramic view of the whole falls and is best visited in the morning when the light is better for photography. The Argentine park (which requires a day to explore properly) offers closer views of the individual falls in their forest setting with its wildlife and butterflies, though to appreciate these properly you need to go early and get well away from the visitors areas. Busiest times are holidays and Sundays. Both parks have visitors' centres and tourist facilities on both sides are constantly being improved.

Parque Nacional Iguazú covers an area of 67,620 ha. The fauna includes jaguars, tapirs, brown capuchin monkeys, collared anteaters and coatimundis, but these are rarely seen around the falls. There is a huge variety of birds; among the butterflies are shiny blue morphos and red/black heliconius. From the Visitor Centre a small gas-run train (free), the **Tren de la Selva**, whisks visitors on a 25-minute trip through the jungle to the Estación del Diablo, where it's a 1-km walk along catwalks across the Río Iguazú to the park's centrepiece, the **Garanta del Diablo**. A visit here is particularly recommended in the evening when the light is best and the swifts are returning to roost on the cliffs, some behind the water. Trains leave on the hour and 30 minutes past the hour. However, it's best to see the falls from a distance first, with excellent views from the two well-organized trails along the **Circuito Superior** and **Circuito Inferior**, each taking around an hour and a half. To reach these, get off the train at the **Estación Cataratas** (after 10 minutes' journey) and walk down the **Sendero Verde**. The Circuito Superior is a level path which takes you along the easternmost line of falls, Bossetti, Bernabé Mandez, Mbiguá (Guaraní for cormorant) and San Martín, allowing you to see these falls from above. This path is safe for

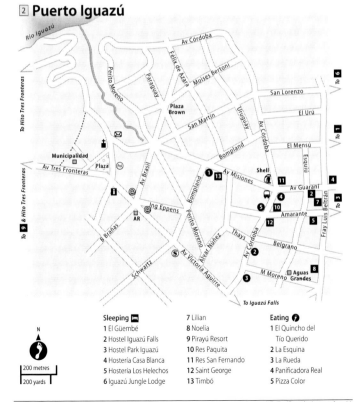

2 Puerto Iguazú

Sleeping
1 El Güembé
2 Hostel Iguazú Falls
3 Hostel Park Iguazú
4 Hostería Casa Blanca
5 Hostería Los Helechos
6 Iguazú Jungle Lodge
7 Lilian
8 Noelia
9 Pirayú Resort
10 Res Paquita
11 Res San Fernando
12 Saint George
13 Timbó

Eating
1 El Quincho del Tío Querido
2 La Esquina
3 La Rueda
4 Panificadora Real
5 Pizza Color

those with walking difficulties, wheelchairs and pushchairs, though you should wear supportive non-slippery shoes. The Circuito Inferior takes you down to the water's edge via a series of steep stairs and walkways with superb views of both San Martín falls and the Gaganta del Diablo from a distance. Wheelchair users, pram pushers, and those who aren't good with steps should go down by the exit route for a smooth and easy descent. You could then return to the Estación Cataratas to take the train to Estación Garganta, 10 and 40 minutes past the hour, and see the falls close up. Every month on the five nights of full moon, there are 1½-hour guided walks (bilingual) that may include or not a dinner afterwards or before the walk, at the Restaurant La Selva, depending on the time of departure. See www.iguazuargentina.com for dates and times. Bookings must be in person at the park, T03757-491469, or through agencies (the Park does not take reservations via email): US$49 with dinner; US$39 without.

At the very bottom of the Circuito Inferior, a free ferry crosses 0930-1530 on demand to the small, hilly **Isla San Martín** where trails lead to *miradores* with good close views of the San Martín falls (last boat back 1630). The park has two further trails: **Sendero Macuco**, 7 km return (allow 6-7 hours), starting from near the Visitor Centre and leading to the river via a natural pool (El Pozón) fed by a slender waterfall, **Salto Arrechea** (a good place for bathing and the only permitted place in the park). **Sendero Yacaratiá** starts from the same place, but reaches the river by a different route, and ends at Puerto Macuco, where you could take the *Jungle Explorer* boat to the see the Falls themselves (see below). This trail is really for vehicles and less pleasant to walk along; better to visit on an organized safari.

Puerto Iguazú → *Phone code: 03757. Population: 81,215.*

This modern town is 18 km northwest of the falls high above the river on the Argentine side near the confluence of the Ríos Iguazú and Alto Paraná. It serves mainly as a centre for visitors to the falls. The port lies to the north of the town centre at the foot of a hill: from the port you can follow the Río Iguazú downstream towards Hito-Tres Fronteras, a *mirador* with views over the point where the Ríos Iguazú and Alto Paraná meet and over neighbouring Brazil and Paraguay. There are souvenir shops, toilets and pubs are here; bus US$0.50. **La Aripuca** ① *T423488, www.aripuca.com.ar, US$3, turn off Ruta 12 just after Hotel Cataratas, entrance after 250 m, English and German spoken*, is a large wooden structure housing a centre for the appreciation of the native tree species and their environment. **Güira Oga** (Casa de los Pájaros) ① *US$2, daily 0830-1800, turn off Ruta 12 at Hotel Orquídeas Palace, entrance is 800 m further along the road from Aripuca; T423980*, is a sanctuary for birds that have been injured, where they are treated and reintroduced to the wild; exquisite parrots and magnificent birds of prey. There is also a trail in the forest and a breeding centre for endangered species.

Iguazú Falls listings

For Sleeping and Eating price codes and other relevant information, see pages 9-10.

🌙 Sleeping

Puerto Iguazú *p42, map p41*

$$$$ Panoramic, Paraguay 372, T498050, www.panoramic-hoteliguazu.com. On a hill overlooking the river, this hotel is stunning. Serene outdoor pool with great views, large well-designed rooms and all 5-star inclusions.

$$$$ Posada Puerto Bemberg, Fundadores Bemberg s/n, Puerto Libertad (some 35 km south of Iguazú), T03757-496500, www.puertobemberg.com. Wonderful luxury accommodation and gourmet cuisine in a 1940s bungalow surrounded by lush gardens. Huge living areas, beautifully decorated rooms and helpful staff. Highly recommended.

$$$$ Sheraton Internacional Iguazú Resort, T491800, www.sheraton.com/iguazu. Fine position overlooking the falls, excellent, good restaurant (dinner buffet US$12) and breakfast, sports facilities and bikes for hire (US$6 for 2 hrs). Taxi to airport US$13. Recommended.

$$$$ Yacutinga Lodge, 30 km from town, pick up by jeep, www.yacutinga.com. A beautiful lodge in the middle of the rainforest, with activities, learning about the bird and plant life and Guaraní culture. Accommodation is in rustic adobe houses in tropical gardens, superb food and drinks included, as well as boat trips and walks. Recommended.

$$$ Iguazú Jungle Lodge, Hipólito Iyrigoyen y San Lorenzo, T420600, www.iguazujungle lodge.com. A well-designed complex of *cabañas* and loft apartments, 7 blocks from the centre, by a river, with lovely pool. Comfortable and stylish, a/c, Wi-Fi, DVDs, great service, breakfast included. Houses sleep 7, good value if full. Warmly recommended.

$$$ Saint George, Córdoba 148, T420633, www.hotelsaintgeorge.com. Comfortable modern-ish rooms around a leafy pool area, with attentive service and a pleasant atmosphere. Insist on an upgraded room. By the bus station. Tours arranged.

$$$ Secret Garden, Los Lapachos 623, T423099, www.secretgardeniguazu.com. Small B&B with attentive owners, fern garden surrounding the house. Spacious rooms, relaxing atmosphere.

$$ Del Parque Ibirá Retá, R12, Km 4, T420872, www.ibirareta.com.ar. Intimate lodge snuggled in the middle of Parque Botánico Ibirá Retá, decorated in simple modern colours, with TV, a/c, breakfast included and there is the option of including dinners as well.

$$ Hostería Casa Blanca, Guaraní 121, near bus station, T421320, www.casablanca iguazu.com.ar. With breakfast, family run, spotless, large rooms, good showers, beautifully maintained.

$$ Pirayú Resort, Av Tres Fronteras 550, on the way to the Hito, T420393, www.pirayu.com.ar. Well-equipped, comfortable *cabañas*, lovely river views, sports and games, pool, entertainment.

$$ Riotropic, C Montecarlo y Av los Inmigrantes, T155 71403, www.riotropic.com.ar. 10 simple but comfortable rooms set around a pool, lovely garden, welcoming. US$5 taxi ride or 20-min walk to town.

$ pp Garden Stone, Av Córdoba 441, T420425, www.gardenstonehostel.com. Lovely new hostel with a homely feel set in nice gardens, with a large outdoor eating area. They have plans for a pool but in the meantime the garden is the perfect place to relax in. Recommended for a tranquil stay.

$ pp Hostel House Las Palmeras, Av Córdoba 341, T425604, info@laspalmeras hostel.com.ar. The cheapest place in town.

Basic rooms, small common area with a pint-sized pool. Good atmosphere. For those on a real budget.

$ pp Hostel Inn Iguazú, R 12, Km 5, T421823, www.hostel-inn.com. 20% discount to HI members and 10% discount on long-distance buses. Large, well-organized hostel which used to be a casino. Huge pool and free internet, pool tables, ping-pong and a range of free DVDs to watch. They also organize package tours to the falls, which include accommodation. Recommended.

$ pp Marco Polo Inn, Av Córdoba 158, T425559, www.hostel-inn.com. The biggest and most central hostel in town, right in front of the bus station. Wi-Fi throughout, nice pool, fun bar at night (open to non-residents). It gets busy so reserve in advance. Recommended.

$ pp Peter Pan, Av Córdoba 267, T423 616, www.peterpanhostel.com. Just down the hill from the bus station, spotless, central pool and large open kitchen. The doubles (**$$**) are lovely. Helpful staff.

$ Timbó Posada, Misiones 147, T422698, www.timboiguazu.com.ar. 100 m from the bus station. Doubles have a/c and Wi-Fi. Kitchen, good breakfasts.

Camping Complejo Americano, Ruta 12, Km 5, T420190, www.complejoamericano.com.ar. 3 pools, wooded gardens, *cabañas* (**$$**), camping US$6 pp, food shop, electricity, barbecue.

Eating

Puerto Iguazú *p42, map p41*

¶¶ Aqva, Av Córdoba y Carlos Thays, T422064. Just down from the bus station, this lovely restaurant serves dishes made with ingredients from the area.

$$ El Quincho del Tío Querido, Bompland 110, T420151. Recommended for *parrilla* and local fish, very popular, great value.

$$ La Esquina, Córdoba 148, next to **Hotel St George**, T425778. Extensive buffet, beef, fish, salads, friendly service.

$$ La Rueda, Córdoba 28, T422531. Good food and prices, fish, steaks and pastas, often with mellow live music. Highly recommended.

$$ Tango Bar Iguazú, Av Brasil 1, T422008. New bar which serves pizzas and pastas. It turns into a milonga with tango classes and dancing at night.

$$-$ Fatto in Casa, Av Brasil 126. Italian food in a lively part of town. Often recommended by locals.

$ Pizza Color, Córdoba y Amarante. Popular for pizza and *parrilla*.

$ Pizzería La Costa, Av Río Iguazú, on costanera. Popular, informal, high above the river on the coast road, looks basic, but the pizzas are superb.

Activities and tours

Iguazú Falls *p40, map p41*
Explorador Expediciones, T421632, www.rainforestevt.com.ar. Offers 2 small-group tours: *Safari a la Cascada* which takes you by jeep to the Arrechea waterfall, stopping along the way to look at wildlife, with a short walk to the falls, 2 hrs, US$20. And *Safari en la Selva,* more in-depth interpretation of the wildlife all around, in open jeeps, 2 hrs, US$28. Highly recommended. They also run birdwatching trips, adventure tours, tours to Moconá.
Jungle Explorer, T421696, www.iguazujunglexplorer.com. Run a series of boat trips, all highly recommended, eg: **Aventura Náutica** is an exhilarating journey by launch along the lower Río Iguazú, from opposite Isla San Martín right up to the San Martín falls and then into the Garganta del Diablo, completely drenching passengers in the mighty spray. Great fun; not for the faint-hearted, 12 mins, US$26. On **Paseo Ecológico** you float silently for 3 km from Estación Garganta to appreciate the wildlife on the river banks, 30 mins, US$15.

Puerto Iguazú *p42, maps p41 and p47*
Agencies arrange day tours to the Brazilian side (lunch in Foz), Itaipú and Ciudad del Este. Some include the Duty Free mall on the Argentine side. Tours to the Jesuit ruins at San Ignacio Miní (US$42 for a full day, but better to stay overnight) also visit a gem mine at Wanda.
Aguas Grandes, Mariano Moreno 58, T425500, www.aguasgrandes.com. Tours to both sides of the falls and further afield, activities in the forest, including half-day for US$28, abseiling down waterfalls, good fun.
Cabalgatas por la Selva, Ruta 12, just after the Rotonda for the road to the international bridge, T155-42180. For horse riding, 3-hr trips, US$23.
Cabalgatas Ecológicas, T154 39763, www.cabalgatasecologicas.com. Good personalized horse-riding tours around Iguazu: 1 hr US$17, 2 hrs US$21.

Transport

Iguazú Falls *p40, map p41*
Bus Transportes El Práctico run every 30 mins from Puerto Iguazú bus terminal, stopping at the park entrance for the purchase of entry tickets, continuing to the Visitor Centre, US$2.50. 1st bus 0700, last 1930, journey time 45 mins; return buses from the park: 0750-2020. You can get on or off the bus at any point en route.

Cars are not allowed beyond visitor centre.

Puerto Iguazú *p42, map p41*
Air Airport is 20 km southeast of Puerto Iguazú near the Falls, T420595. A bus service between airport and bus terminal connects with plane arrivals and departures, US$5, will also drop off/collect you from your hotel. **AR/Austral** and **LAN** fly direct to **Buenos Aires**, 1 hr 40 mins.

Bus The bus terminal, at Av Córdoba y Av Misiones, T421916, has a phone office, restaurant, various tour company desks and bus offices. To **Buenos Aires**, 16-18 hrs, Tigre Iguazú, Via Bariloche and others, daily, US$90-103. To **Posadas**, stopping at San Ignacio Miní, frequent, 5-6 hrs, US$14.75-21, *expreso*; to **San Ignacio Miní**, US$11, *servicio común*. **Agencia de Pasajes Noelia**, local 3, T422722, can book tickets beyond Posadas for other destinations in Argentina, ISIC discounts available.

Taxi T420973/421707.

Border with Brazil
Crossing via the Puente Tancredo Neves is straight-forward. When leaving Argentina, Argentine immigration is at the Brazilian end of the bridge. Border open 0700-2300.
Brazilian consulate, Av Córdoba 278, T420192.

Bus Leave Puerto Iguazú terminal for Foz do Iguaçu every 20 mins, US$2. The bus stops at the Argentine border post, but not the Brazilian. Both Argentine and Brazilian officials stamp you in and out, even if only for a day visit. Whether you are entering Brazil for the first time, or leaving and returning after a day in Argentina, you must insist on getting off the bus to get the requried stamp and entry card. Buses also stop at the Duty Free mall. The bus does not wait for those who need stamps, just catch the next one, of whatever company. **Taxis** Between the border and Puerto Iguazú US$20.

Border with Paraguay
Crossing to Paraguay is via Puente Tancredo Neves to Brazil and then via the Puente de la Amistad to Ciudad del Este. Brazilian entry and exit stamps are not required unless you are stopping in Brazil. US$4 charge to enter Paraguay. The **Paraguayan consulate** is at Puerto Moreno 236, T424230, 0800-1500.

Bus Direct buses (non-stop in Brazil), leave Puerto Iguazú terminal every 30 mins, US$2.75, 45 mins, liable to delays especially in crossing the bridge to Ciudad del Este. Only one bus on Sun, no schedule, better to go to Foz and change buses there.

Directory

Puerto Iguazú p42, map p41
Airline offices Aerolíneas Argentinas, Brasil y Aguirre, T420168. **Andes**, Av Victoria Aguirre 283, T425566. **LAN** T0810-999 9526.

Banks ATMs at **Macro**, Misiones y Bonpland, and **Banco de la Nación**, Av Aguirre 179. *Sheraton* has an ATM. TCs can only be changed at **Libres Cambio** in the Hito Tres Fronteras, 0800-2200. Good exchange rates at the Brazilian border. **Internet** Generally expensive, US$1-1.20 per hr. Several places in town.

Brazil side of the falls

Ins and outs
Tourist offices Foz do Iguaçu: Secretaria Municipal de Turismo ⓘ *Praça Getúlio Vargas 69, T3521 1455, 0700-2300, www.fozdoiguacu.pr.gov.br.* Very helpful, English spoken. There is a 24-hour tourist help line number, T0800-451516. Very helpful. Airport tourist information is also good, open for all arriving flights, gives map and bus information, English spoken. Helpful office, free map, at the rodoviária, daily 0630-1800, English spoken. Also at the Terminal de Transporte Urbano, daily 0700-1800.

Parque Nacional Foz do Iguaçu
ⓘ *US$23.25, payable in reais, Argentine pesos, euros or dollars, includes obligatory transport within the park (discounts for Mercosur, Brazilian and local residents). The park is open daily, 0900-1700 in winter, and to 1800 in summer; T3521 4400, www.cataratasdoiguacu.com.br.*
The Brazilian national park was founded in 1939 and the area was designated a World Heritage Site by UNESCO in 1986. Fauna most frequently encountered are little and red brocket deer, South American coati, white-eared opossum, and a sub-species of the brown capuchin monkey. The endangered tegu lizard is common. Over 100 species of butterflies have been identified, among them the electric blue Morpho, the poisonous red and black heliconius and species of Papilionidae and Pieridae. The bird life is rewarding for bird-watchers. Five members of the toucan family can be seen.

Take a bus or taxi to the park's entrance, Km 21 from Foz. There's a smart modern **visitor centre** here, with toilets, ATM, a small café, a large souvenir shop and a Banco do Brasil câmbio (1300-1700). An **Exposição Ecológica** has information about the natural history of the falls and surrounding park (included in entry fee; English texts poor). Nature lovers are advised to visit first thing in the morning or late in the afternoon, preferably in low season, as crowds can significantly detract from the experience of the falls and surrounding park (at peak times like Semana Santa up to 10,000 visitors a day arrive). From the entrance, shuttle buses leave every 10-15 minutes for the 10 km to the start of the Cascades Trail, another 1 km to the end of the road at Porta Canoas. There are Portuguese, Spanish and English announcements of the stops (each bus will carry three bikes). The bus stops first at the start of the **Macuco Safari** (see page 51). From there it continues to the Hotel das Cataratas and the start of a 1.5 km paved walk to the falls. This is an easy walk, taking you high above the Rio Iguaçu, giving splendid views of all the falls on the Argentine side from a series of galleries. At the end of the path, you can walk down to a boardwalk at the foot of the Floriano Falls which goes almost to the middle of the river to give a good view of and a light spraying from the Garganta del Diablo. There is also a viewing point almost under the powerful Floriano Falls, a dramatic view. From here, there are 150 steps up to the **Porto Canoas** complex (there is a lift for those who find stairs difficult); you can also return the way you came, and walk a little further along the road. The Porto Canoas complex consists of a big souvenir shop, toilets, a café, a fast food place (mixed reports) and smart **restaurant** ① *buffet lunch for US$22.50, 1200-1600, good value*, all with good view of the river above the falls. Return to the visitor centre and entrance either by the free shuttle bus, or by walking back as far as Hotel das Cataratas (good lunch with a view of the falls) and taking the bus from there. The whole visit will take around two hours, plus time for lunch. Never feed wild animals and keep your distance when taking photos; coatis have been known to attack visitors with food.

Foz do Iguaçu

Sleeping
1 Arterial
2 Baviera
3 Del Rey
4 Foz do Iguaçu
5 Foz Plaza
6 Foz Presidente
7 Luz
8 Pousada da Laura
9 Rafain Centro
10 San Juan Centro
11 San Remo
12 Suiça
13 Tarobá

Eating
1 Atos
2 Bier Garten
3 Búfalo Branco
4 City Caffé
5 Marias e Maria
6 Oficina do Sorvete
7 Rafain
8 Tropicana
9 Zaragoza

Bars & clubs
10 Alquimia
11 Armazém
12 BR3
13 Capitão
14 Oba! Oba!

Foz do Iguaçu and around → *Phone code: 0xx45. Population: 301,400.*
A small, modern city, 28 km from the falls, with a wide range of accommodation and good communications by air and road with the main cities of southern Brazil and Asunción in Paraguay. The **Parque das Aves bird zoo** ⓘ *Rodovia das Cataratas Km 16, 100 m before the entrance to the falls, T3529 8282, www.parquedasaves.com.br, 0830-1730, US$15*, has received frequent good reports. It contains Brazilian and foreign birds, many species of parrot and beautiful toucans, in huge aviaries through which you can walk, with the birds flying and hopping around you. There are other birds in cages and a butterfly and hummingbird house.

The **Itaipu dam** ⓘ *on the Río Paraná 12 km north, a short film is shown at the visitor centre 10 mins before each guided visit, there are short bus tours, US$11.75, full tours including the interior of the dam: 8 departures daily between 0800 and 1600, US$31 and night views, Fri-Sat 2000, US$7.40, children and seniors half price for all visits, check times with tourist office, take passport and wear long trousers and sensible shoes, best light for photography in the morning, T0800-645 4645, www.itaipu.gov.br, www.turismoitaipu.com.br*, is the site of the largest single power station in the world, built jointly by Brazil and Paraguay. Construction of this massive scheme began in 1975 and it became operational in 1984. The main dam is 8 km long, creating a lake which covers 1400 sq km. The 18 turbines have an installed capacity of 12,600,000 Kw and produce about 75 bn Kwh a year, providing 80% of Paraguay's electricity and 25% of Brazil's. The Paraguayan side may be visited from Ciudad del Este. Several beaches can be visited around the lake. A large reforestation project is underway and six biological refuges have been created on the lakeshore in both countries. There is also the **Ecomuseu de Itaipu** ⓘ *Av Tancredo Neves, Km 11, T0800-645 4645, Tue-Sun 0830-1730, US$4.90, closed for renovations until Dec 2011*, and **Refúgio Bela Vista** ⓘ *closed Tue, 4 visits a day from the visitor centre, US$11*, animal rescue centre and home to the fauna displaced by the dam, both geared to educate about the preservation of the local culture and environment, or that part which isn't underwater. Recommended. In addition there is the **Polo Astronômico** ⓘ *T3576 7203, Wed-Sun at 0930 and 1530, Fri-Sat also 1900, US$9.25, www.pti.org.br/turismo/polo-astronomico*, a planetarium and astronomical observatory.

Border with Argentina

All foreigners must get exit and entry stamps both in Brazil and Argentina every time they cross the border, even if it is only for the day. It is your responsibility to get the stamps, if riding a taxi make shure it stops at both border posts, if riding a city bus, ask for a transfer, get off at the Brazilian border post and get on the next bus through without paying again. If entering Brazil, be sure you also get the entry card stamped.

Between October-February Brazil is one hour ahead of Argentina. It takes about two hours to get from Foz to the Argentine falls, very tiring when the weather is hot.

Border with Paraguay → *Brazil is 1 hr ahead of Paraguay.*

The Ponte de Amizade/Puente de Amistad (Friendship Bridge) over the Río Paraná, 6 km north of Foz, leads straight into the heart of Ciudad del Este. Paraguayan and Brazilian immigration formalities (open until 1700) are dealt with at opposite ends of the bridge. Ask for relevant stamps if you need them. A large new customs complex has been built at the Brazilian end of the bridge. The area is intensively patrolled for contraband and stolen cars; ensure that all documentation is in order.

Foz do Iguaçu listings

For Sleeping and Eating price codes and other relevant information, see pages 9-10.

Sleeping

Foz do Iguaçu *p48, map p47*
Note Check hotels' websites for internet prices and special offers. Av Juscelino Kubitschek and the streets south of it, towards the river, are unsafe at night. Many prostitutes around R Rebouças and Almirante Barroso. Taxis are only good value for short distances when you are carrying all your luggage.

$$$$ Suíça, Av Felipe Wandscheer 3580, T3025 3232, www.hotelsuica.com.br. Some way out of the city, comfortable, Swiss manager, helpful with tourist information, attractive pools, gym.

$$$$-$$ Luz, Av Costa e Silva Km 5, near Rodoviária, T3522 3535, www.luzhotel. com.br. A/c, buffet restaurant, TV, pool. Recommended.

$$$ Baviera, Av Jorge Schimmelpfeng 697, T3523 5995, www.hotelbavieraiguassu.com.br. Chalet-style exterior, on main road, central for bars and restaurants, comfortable, if rather gloomy rooms.

$$$ Del Rey, R Tarobá 1020, T2105 7500, www.hoteldelreyfoz.com.br. Nothing fancy, but perennially popular, little pool, great breakfasts, Wi-Fi. Recommended.

$$$ Foz do Iguaçu, Av Brasil 97, T3521 4455, www.hotelfozdoiguacu.com.br. Attractive pool and terrace, well-designed but faded rooms.

$$$ Foz Plaza, R Marechal Deodoro 1819, T3521 5500, www.fozplazahotel.com.br. Serene and very nice, restaurant, Wi-Fi, pool.

$$$ Foz Presidente I, R Xavier da Silva 1000 and **II** at R Mcal Floriano Peixoto 1851, T3572 4450, www.fozpresidentehoteis.com.br. Good value, with breakfast, decent rooms, restaurant, pool. Number 1 is convenient for buses, Wi-Fi.

$$$ San Juan Tour, R Marechal Deodoro 1349, T2105 9100, www.sanjuanhoteis.com.br. cheaper if booked on-line. A/c, comfortable, excellent buffet breakfast, popular, good value. Recommended. The more expensive **San Juan Eco** is on the road to the falls.

$$$ Tarobá, R Tarobá 1048, T2102 7770, www.hotel taroba.com.br. In Best Western chain, bright and welcoming, small pool, nice rooms, helpful, a/c, good breakfast (extra), Wi-Fi, good value.

$$ Pousada da Laura, R Naipi 671, T3572 3374. **$** pp in shared dorm with good breakfast. Secure, kitchen, laundry facilities, internet, Wi-Fi, a popular place to meet other travellers.

$$ Pousada El Shaddai, R Rebouças 306, near Terminal Urbana, T3025 4493, www.pousadaelshaddai.com.br. Includes buffet breakfast, a/c, cheaper with fan and shared bath, **$** pp in dorm, pool, internet.

$$ San Remo, Xavier da Silva 563 at Tarobá, T3523 1619, roberto_171@hotmail.com. Scrupulously clean though small rooms with TV, all you can eat breakfast, English, Spanish and Hebrew spoken. In-house travel agency.

$ Arterial, Av José Maria de Brito 2661, T3573 1859, hotelarterial@hotmail.com. Near rodoviária. Good value, huge breakfast, cable TV, a/c, opposite is a 24-hr buffet restaurant.

$ Hostel Bambu, R Edmundo de Barros 621, T3523 3646, www.hostelbambu.com. Central hostel with a pool, outdoor bar, Wi-Fi, use of kitchen and tours organized.

$ Pousada Evelina, R Irlan Kalichewski 171, Vila Yolanda, T3574 3817, www.pousada evelina.com.br. Lots of tourist information, English, French, Italian, Polish and Spanish spoken, internet, good breakfast and location, near Chemin Supermarket, near Av Cataratas on the way to the falls. Recommended.

Camping Camping e Pousada **Internacional**, R Manêncio Martins 21, 1.5 km from town, T3529 8183, www.camping internacional.com.br. For vehicles and tents, US$15 pp (half with International Camping Card), also basic cabins (**$**), helpful staff,

English, German and Spanish spoken, pool, restaurant. **Note** Camping is not permitted by the Hotel das Cataratas and falls.

Outside Foz do Iguaçu
$$$$ Hotel das Cataratas, directly overlooking the Falls, Km 32 from Foz, T2102 7000, www.hotel dascataratas.com. Generally recommended but caters for lots of groups, attractive colonial-style building with pleasant gardens (where wildlife can be seen at night and early morning) and pool. Non-residents can eat here, midday and evening buffets; also à-la-carte dishes and dinner with show. Member of the Orient Express group.

On the road to the falls (Rodovia das Cataratas) are:
$$$$ San Martin, Km 17, T3521 8088, www.hotelsanmartin.com.br. Attractive 4-star, a/c, TV, Wi-Fi, pool, sports, nightclub, several eating options, luxury, comfortable, lots of packages offered. Recommended.
$$$ Carimã, Km 10, T3521 3000, www.hotel carima.com.br. 4-star, popular with groups, well laid out, lots of facilities, good restaurant, pool, bars, good value.
$$$-$$ Hostel Natura, Rodovia das Cataratas Km 12.5, Remanso Grande, T3529 6949, www.hostelnatura.com (near the Paudimar). Rustic hostel with a small pool set in fields. Rooms with fan, **$** pp in dorm, **$** pp to camp, pool table, TV lounge, small kitchen, arrange visits to the falls; website has detailed instructions for how to reach them.
$$-$ Paudimar Campestre, Av das Cataratas Km 12.5, Remanso Grande, near airport, T3529 6061, www.paudimar.com.br. In high season HI members only. From airport or town take Parque Nacional bus (0525-0040) and get out at Remanso Grande bus stop, by Hotel San Juan Eco, then take the free shuttle (0700-1900) to the hostel, or 1.2 km walk from main road. Camping as well (**$**), pool, soccer pitch, quiet, kitchen and communal meals, breakfast. Highly recommended. For assistance, ask for owner, Gladis. The hostel has telephone, fax and internet for guests' use. Tours run to either side of the falls (good value). Paudimar desk at rodoviária.

● Eating

Foz do Iguaçu p48, map p47
Plenty of places here serve Middle Eastern food.
$$$ Búfalo Branco, R Rebouças 530, T3523 9744. Superb all you can eat churrasco, includes filet mignon, bull's testicles, salad bar and desert. Sophisticated surroundings and attentive service. Highly recommended.
$$$ Cabeça de Boi, Av Felipe Wandscheer, Km 6, T3525 3358. Live music, buffet, churrasco, but coffee and pastries also.
$$$ Rafain, Av das Cataratas, Km 6.5, T3523 1177. Closed Sun. Out of town, take a taxi or arrange with travel agency. Set price for excellent buffet with folkloric music and dancing (2100-2300), touristy but very entertaining.
$$$ Zaragoza, R Quintino Bocaiúva 882, T3574 3084. Large and upmarket, for Spanish dishes and seafood. Recommended.
$$ Atos, Av Juscelino Kubitschek 865, T3572 2785. Per kilo buffet with various meats, salads, sushi and puddings. Lunch only.
$$ Bier Garten, Av Jorge Schimmelpfeng 550, T3523 3700. Bustling pizzeria, churrascaria and choperia.
$ Iguassu Âgape, R Marechal Deodoro 1819, T3521 5544. Good value per kilo place next to Hotel Foz Plaza. *Feijoada* on Sat.

Cafés
Marias e Maria, Av Brasil 505. Good confeitaria.
Oficina do Sorvete, Av Jorge Schimmelpfeng 244. Daily 1100-0100. Excellent ice creams, a popular local hang-out.

● Bars and clubs

Foz do Iguaçu p48, map p47
Bars, all doubling as restaurants, concentrated on Av Jorge Schimmelpfeng for 2 blocks from Av Brasil to R Mal Floriano Peixoto. Wed to Sun are best nights; crowd tends to be young.

Armazém, R Edmundo de Barros 446, T3572 7422. Intimate and sophisticated, attracts discerning locals, good atmosphere, mellow live music, US$1 cover. Recommended.
Capitão Bar, Av Jorge Schimmelpfeng 288 and Almte Barroso, T3572 1512. Large, loud and popular, nightclub attached.
Oba! Oba!, Av das Cataratas 3700, T529 6596 (Antigo Castelinho). Live samba show Mon-Sat 2315-0015, very popular, US$12 including drink.
Pizza Park Bar, R Almirante Barroso 993. Specialises in vodka and whisky brands. Wi-Fi zone.

Activities and tours

Parque Nacional Foz do Iguaçu p46
Tours
Macuco Safari, T3529 6262, or 9963.3857, www.macucosafari.com.br, 2 hrs, US$100, involves a ride down a 1½-km path through the forest in open jeeps and an optional walk. Then a fast motor boat whisks you close to the falls themselves (similar to Jungle Explorer on the Argentine side, but more expensive and the guides aren't as good). Portuguese, English and Spanish spoken, take insect repellent and waterproof camera bag.
Helicopter tours over the falls leave from near the entrance, US$100 pp, 10 mins. Apart from disturbing visitors, they disturb bird life and so the altitude has been increased, making the flight less attractive. Lots of companies on both sides organize **conventional tours** to the falls, useful more for convenience rather than information, since they collect you from your hotel. Half day, US$13, plus park entrance price.

Foz do Iguaçu p48, map p47
Tours
There are many travel agents on Av Brasil. Beware of overcharging by touts at the bus terminal.
Caribe Tur at the airport, Hotel das Cataratas and other branches, T3529 7505, www.grupo caribe.com.br, runs tours from the airport to the Argentine side and Hotel das Cataratas (book hotel direct, not at the airport).
RD Falls, Av Costa E Silva 451, Iguaçu International Bus Terminal, office 10, T3027 4157, http://rdfalls.com/en. Offers day trips to the Iguazu Falls for Foz and various other tours.
STTC Turismo, Av Iguaçu 873, T3026 3001, www.sttceventoseturismo.com.br. Ruth Campo Silva (recommended guide). Several branches.

Transport

Parque Nacional Foz do Iguaçu p46
Bus Leave from the Terminal Urbana in Foz, Av Juscelino Kubitschek and República Argentina, every 40 mins from 0730-1800, and are clearly marked 'Parque Nacional'. You can get on or off at any point on the route past the airport and Hotel das Cataratas, 40 mins, US$1.50 one way, payable in reais or pesos (bus route ends at the Park entrance where you purchase entry tickets and change to a park bus). Taxi US$20, negotiate in advance the return trip.

Foz do Iguaçu p48, map p47
Air Aeroporto Internacional de Cataratas, BR 469, Km 16.5, 13 km east of the centre and 12 km from the falls, T3521 4200. In Arrivals is **Banco do Brasil** and **Caribe Tours e Câmbio**, car rental offices, tourist office and an official taxi stand, US$22 to town centre. All buses marked Parque Nacional pass the airport in each direction, US$1.50, 0525-0040, does not permit large amounts of luggage but backpacks OK. Many hotels run minibus services for a small charge. Daily flights to **Rio, São Paulo, Curitiba** and other Brazilian cities.

Bus For transport to the falls see above under Parque Nacional Foz do Iguaçu.
Rodoviária long distance terminal , Av Costa e Silva, 4 km from centre on road to Curitiba, T3522 3633; bus to centre from next to the taxis, US$1.20. Taxi US$8. Book departures as soon as possible. As well as the tourist office, there is a Cetreme desk for tourists who have

lost their documents, Guarda Municipal (police), Visa ATM, and luggage store. To **Curitiba**, Catarinense, Pluma, 9-10 hrs, paved road, US$50. To **Guaíra** via Cascavel only, 5 hrs, US$20. To **Florianópolis**, Catarinense (www.catarinense.net) and Reunidas, US$55, 14 hrs. **Reunidas** to **Porto Alegre**, US$58-66. To **São Paulo**, 16 hrs, Pluma US$50, 1 *convencional*, 1 *leito*; also has 2 daily to **Rio** 22 hrs, US$83. To **Campo Grande**, US$59. Local buses leave from the **Terminal de Transporte Urbano, TTU** on Av Juscelino Kubitscheck. **Green Toad Bus**, Av Costa E Silva 451, Iguaçu International Bus Terminal, office 10, T8610 6974, www.greentoadbus.com.

Foz do Iguaçu and around: Itaipu dam *p48*
Bus Take bus lines Conjunto C Norte or Conjunto C Sul from Foz do Iguaçu Terminal de Transporte Urbano, US$1.50. The Noelia company in Puerto Iguazú includes Itaipu in its tours of the falls, T422722.

Border with Argentina: Foz do Iguaçu/ Puerto Iguazú *p48*
Bus Marked 'Puerto Iguazú' run every 30 mins Mon-Sat, hourly on Sun, from the Terminal Urbana, crossing the border bridge; 30 mins' journey, 3 companies, US$2.50. See above for procedures regarding entry stamps. **Note** Be sure you know when the last bus departs from Puerto Iguazú for Foz (usually 1900); last bus from Foz 1950. If visiting the Brazilian side for a day, get off the bus at the Hotel Bourbon, cross the road and catch the bus to the Falls, rather than going into Foz and out again. Combined tickets to Puerto Iguazú and the falls cost more than paying separately. For buses to **Buenos Aires**, see Puerto Iguazú, Transport for the options. There is a Pluma bus direct from Foz, 1830 Tue, Thu, Sat, and you can also go to Posadas via Paraguay.

Border with Paraguay: Foz do Iguaçu/ Ciudad del Este *p48*
Bus (Marked Cidade-Ponte) leave from the Terminal Urbana, Av Juscelino Kubitschek, for the Ponte de Amizade (Friendship Bridge), US$0.75. To **Asunción**, Pluma (0700), RYSA (direct at 1430, 1830), from Rodoviária, US$16.50-20 (cheaper from Ciudad del Este).

Car If crossing by private vehicle and only intending to visit the national parks, this presents no problems. Another crossing to Paraguay is at **Guaíra**, at the northern end of the Itaipu lake. It is 5 hrs north of Iguaçu by road and can be reached by bus from Campo Grande and São Paulo. Ferries cross to Saltos del Guaira on the Paraguayan side.

Directory

Foz do Iguaçu *p48, map p47*
Airline offices Gol, at airport, T3521 4230, or 0300-115 2121. Ocean Air, at airport, T3521 4256. **TAM**, R Rio Branco 640, T3523 8500 (offers free transport to Ciudad del Este for its flights, all cross-border documentation dealt with). **Banks** It is difficult to exchange on Sun but quite possible in Paraguay where US dollars can be obtained on credit cards. There are plenty of banks and travel agents on Av Brasil. Banco do Brasil, Av Brasil 1377. ATM, high commission for TCs. Bradesco, Av Brasil 1202. Cash advance on Visa. HSBC, Av Brasil 1151, for MasterCard ATM. Banco 24 Horas at Oklahoma petrol station. Câmbio at Vento Sul, Av Brasil 1162, no TCs, good rates for cash. Also Corimeira, Av Brasil 148. **Embassies and consulates** Argentina, Travessa Eduardo Bianchi 26, T3574 2969. Mon-Fri 1000-1500. France, R Ernesto Keller 995, Jardim Eliza II, T3529 6850, 0900-1230. Paraguay, R Marechal Deodoro 901, T3523 2898, Mon-Thu 0830-1530, Fri 0830-1500. **Medical services** Free 24-hr clinic, Av Paraná 1525, opposite Lions Club, T3521 1850. Few buses: take taxi or walk (about 25 mins). **Post offices** Praça Getúlio Vargas 72. **Telephones** Several call centres.

Región Oriental: South of Asunción

Ruta 1 runs south from Asunción to Encarnación and the Argentine border. This is an attractive area of fertile landscapes, sleepy towns and the historically important Jesuits settlements, the ruins of some of which have been restored and now have interpretive and even multimedia exhibits.

Itá (Km 37) is famous for rustic pottery, but also sells wood, leather and textile items including hammocks. You can visit the workshop of **Rosa Brítez**, a local ceramics artist and Paraguay's most famous artisan, recognized by UNESCO. Its church, San Blas, was built in 1585 and the town has a lagoon which is reputed never to dry up.

Yaguarón
Founded in 1539, Yaguarón, Km 48, was the centre of the Franciscan missions in colonial times. At the centre of the town, marooned on an island of green, mown grass, stands the church of **San Buenaventura**, with its external bell-tower ① *daily 0700-1100, 1330-1630, on Sun morning only*. The simplicity and symmetry of the exterior is matched by the ornate carvings and paintings of the interior. The tints, made by the *indígenas* from local plants, are still bright on the woodcarvings and the angels have Guaraní faces. Built in Hispano-Guaraní Baroque style by the Franciscans between 1755 and 1772, it was reconstructed in 1885 and renovated in the late 20th century. Stations of the Cross behind the village lead to a good view of the surroundings.

 Museo Dr José Gaspar Rodríguez de Francia ① *leaving the church, 500 m down the road to your left, Tue-Sun 0730-1130, free guided tour in Spanish*, with artefacts from the life of Paraguay's first dictator, 'El Supremo', plus paintings and artefacts from the 18th century. The 18th-century single-storey adobe building with bamboo ceilings and tiled roof belonged to Francia's father. The fiesta patronal, San Buenaventura, is in mid-July. There are a few basic hotels (**$**).

Paraguarí and around → *Phone code: 531. Population: 23,335.*
Founded 1775 and located at Km 63 along Ruta 1, this is the north entrance to the mission area, at the foot of a range of hills. Its restored church has two bell towers, separate from the main structure. Buses between Asunción and Encarnación stop here. There is an interesting Artillery Museum inside the nearby military base with cannons and artefacts from the Chaco War. You can stroll to the top of Cerro Perõ for views from the cross on top. More challenging is a one-hour climb through dense forest to the summit of Cerro Jhu, ask for directions in Barrio San Miguel behind the abandoned train station. Paraguarí retains many customs from its Spanish founders, and is seen as Paraguay's capital of bullfighting.

 Sapucaí, 25 km east of Paraguarí, the terminus of the tourist train from Asunción, is the location of the **workshops** ① *Mon-Fri, take a bus from Asunción at 0700, 1200, 88 km, 3 hrs, US$1.25*, where you can see old and abandoned wood-burning steam locomotives. There are also some *hospedajes* (**$**).

Northeast from Paraguarí 15 km is **Chololó** ① *bus US$0.55*, with a small but attractive series of waterfalls and rapids with bathing facilities and walkways, mainly visited in the summer.

Parque Nacional Ybycuí

At **Carapeguá**, Km 84 (*hospedaje* on main street, basic, friendly; blankets and hammocks to rent along the main road, or buy your own, made locally and cheaper than elsewhere), a road turns off to Acahay, Ybycuí and the **Parque Nacional Ybycuí** ① *0800-1700, www.salvemoslos.com.py/pny.htm. For camping get a permit from the Environmental Department, Madame Lynch 3500, in Asunción (see National parks, page 7)*, 67 km southeast. This is one of the most accessible national parks, if you have a car, and is one of the few remaining areas of rainforest in eastern Paraguay. It contains 5000 ha of virgin forest and was founded in 1973. Good walks, a beautiful campsite and lots of waterfalls. At the entrance is a well set out park and museum, plus the reconstructed remains of the country's first iron foundry (La Rosada). Crowded on Sunday but deserted the rest of the week. Guides available. The only shops (apart from a small one at the entrance selling drinks, eggs, etc, and a good T-shirt stall which helps support the park) are at **Ybycuí**, 30 km northwest.

Ruta 1 continues through **Villa Florida**, 162 km from Asunción, on the banks of the Río Tebicuary. It's a popular spot in January-February for its sandy beaches and the fishing is first-rate. The Hotel Nacional de Villa Florida (**$**, T083-240207), one of three such places run by Senatur (see also Vapor Cué, page 33 and Ayolas, below, www.paraguay.gov.py) would make a convenient place to stop when travelling on this route.

The Jesuit missions

In 1578 Jesuit missionaries came to what is now the border region of Brazil, Argentina and Paraguay to convert the Guaraníes to Christianity. The first mission was established in 1609 at San Ignacio Guazú. Together these two groups developed a pioneering economic and social system that emphasized collaboration and, to some extent, integration between the two societies. In 1767, by decree of Charles III of Spain, the Jesuits were expelled and local wealthy landowners took the Guaraníes as slave workers. Thirty missions, or *reducciones*, were built. Eight of these remain in Paraguay in varying states of repair and three have been inscribed as UNESCO World Heritage Sites. See *The Mission*, Films, in Background.

San Ignacio Guazú and around

At Km 226, this is a delightful town on the site of a former Jesuit *reducción* (*guazú* means big in Guaraní). Several typical Hispano-Guaraní buildings survive. Each Sunday night at 2000 a folklore festival is held in the central plaza, free, very local, "fabulous". The **Museo Jesuítico** ① *daily 0800-1130, 1400-1730, US$1*, housed in the former Jesuit art workshop, reputedly the oldest surviving civil building in Paraguay, contains a major collection of Guaraní art and sculpture from the missionary period. The attendant is very knowledgeable, but photos are not allowed. Nearby is the **Museo Histórico Sembranza de Héroes** ① *Mon-Sat 0745-1145, 1400-1700, Sun 0800-1100*, with displays on the Chaco War. For tours of the area or to visit local ranches contact Emi Tours, T078-220286.

Santa María de Fé is 12 km northeast along a cobbled road. Here there is another fine museum ① *0900-1300, 1500-1800, US$0.40 (photos allowed)*, in restored mission buildings containing 60 Guaraní sculptures among the exhibits. The modern church has a lovely altarpiece of the Virgin and Child (the key is kept at a house on the opposite side of the plaza). There is also the **Santa María Cooperative and Educational Fund**, begun by English journalist Margaret Hebblethwaite, which sponsors education and craftwork (notably appliqué) and organizes local activities for visitors. Santa María de Fé was between 1960-1976 the home of the radically utopian **Ligas Agrarias Cristianas** (Christian Agrarian League) until forcibly suppressed by Stroessner. There is a hotel on the plaza, see www.santamaria hotel.org and www.santamariadefe.org.

At **Santa Rosa** (Km 248), founded 1698, only a chapel of the original Jesuit church survived a fire. The chapel houses a museum; on the walls are frescoes in poor condition; exhibits include a sculpture of the Annunciation considered to be one of the great works of the Hispanic American Baroque (ask at the parroquia next door for entry). Daily buses from San Ignacio Guazú.

Southwest to Pilar Ruta 4 (paved) from San Ignacio (see above) goes southwest to **Pilar** (*phone code: 086*; hotels in **$** range), on the banks of the Río Paraguay. Capital of Neembucú district, the town is known for its fishing, manufacturing and historical Cabildo. This area saw many bloody battles during the War of the Triple Alliance and you can visit **Humaitá**, with the old church of San Carlos, **Paso de Patria**, **Curupayty** and other historic battle sites.

Ayolas, Santiago and San Cosme

At Km 262 on Ruta 1 a road leads to the *reducción* at Santiago and the town of **Ayolas** standing on the banks of the Aña Cuá river. **Santiago** is another important Jesuit centre (founded 1669) with a modern church containing a fine wooden carving of Santiago slaying the Saracens. More wooden statuary in the small museum next door (ask around the village for the key-holder). There is an annual **Fiesta de la Tradición Misionera**, 2-3 February. Beyond is **Ayolas**, good for fishing and influenced by the construction of the Yacyretá dam. There is an archaeological museum and, 12 km from Ayolas, the **Refugio Faunístico de Atinguy** ⓘ *Mon-Sat 0830-1130 and 1330-1630, Sun and holidays 0830-1130*, run as a research and educational facility by the **Entidad Binacional Yacyretá** (EBY) to study the fauna affected by the dam. EBY also has a biological reserve on the **island of Yacyretá** itself ⓘ *visits to the project at 0830, 1000, 1400, T072-222141, or 021-445055, www.eby.gov.py*. Cross the river to Ituzaingó, Argentina (linked via road to Corrientes and Posadas). Follow the unpaved road from Ayolas to the **San Cosme y Damián** *reducciones* or leave Ruta 1 at Km 306. When the Jesuits were expelled from Spanish colonies in 1767, the **church and ancillary buildings** ⓘ *0700-1130, 1300-1700 US$1*, were unfinished. A huge project has followed the original plans. Some of the *casas de indios* are still in use (for other purposes).

Encarnación → *Phone code: 071. Population: 93,497.*

A bridge connects this busy port, the largest town in the region (founded 1614), with the Argentine town of Posadas across the Alto Paraná. The old town was badly neglected at one time as it was due to be flooded when the Yacyretá-Apipé dam was completed. Since the flooding, however, what is not under water has been restored and a modern town has been built higher up. This is less interesting than the lower part, once the main commercial area selling a wide range of cheap goods to visitors from Argentina and Brazil. The town exports the products of a rich area: timber, soya, mate, tobacco, cotton, and hides; it is fast losing its traditional, rural appearance. The town is a good base for visiting nearby Jesuit mission sites. Given its proximity to the border, the cost of living is higher than in most other parts of Paraguay. The **tourist office** ⓘ *by Universidad Católica, T204515, 0800-1200*, is very helpful and has a street map. In the afternoon maps are available from the Municipalidad, Estigarribia y Kreusser, Oficina de Planificación.

Border with Argentina
The San Roque road bridge connects Encarnación with **Posadas**. Formalities are conducted at respective ends of the bridge. Argentine side has different offices for locals and foreigners; Paraguay has one for both. **Note** Paraguay is one hour behind Argentina, except during Paraguayan summer time (October-April).

Santísima Trinidad del Paraná and Jesús de Tavarangüé
Northeast from Encarnación along Ruta 6 towards Ciudad del Este are the two best-preserved Jesuit *reducciones*, see box, page . These are both recognized as UNESCO World Cultural Heritage sites (whc.unesco. org/en/list/648). The hilltop site of **Trinidad** ⓘ *US$3, Oct-May 0700-1900, Apr-Sep 0700-1730*, built 1706-1760, has undergone significant restoration. Note the partially restored church, the carved stone pulpit, the font and other masonry and relief sculpture. Also partially rebuilt is the bell-tower near the original church (great views from the top). You can also see another church, a college, workshops and indigenous living quarters. It was founded in 1706 by Padre Juan de Anaya; the architect was Juan Bautista Prímoli. For information or tours (in Spanish and German), ask at the visitor centre; ongoing restoration efforts may mean some missions are closed. The Jesuito Snack Bar at the turn off from the main road has decent food. 1 km from Trinidad is **Ita Cajón**, an enormous clearing where the stone was quarried for the Jesuit *reducción*.

About 10 km northwest of Trinidad, along a rough road (which turns off 300 m north from Trinidad entrance) is **Jesús de Tavarangüé**, now a small town where another group of Jesuits settled in 1763. In the less than four years before they were expelled they embarked on a huge

Encarnación

Sleeping
Acuario 1
Central 2
Cristal 3
Encarnación Resort 4
Germano 5
Itapúa 6
Liz 7
Paraná 8
Viena 9

construction programme that included the church, sacristy, residencia and baptistry, on one side of which is a square tower ① *Oct-May 0700-1900, Apr-Sep 0700-1730, US$3*. There is a fine front façade with three great arched portals in a Moorish style. The ruins have been restored. There are beautiful views from the main tower.

German colonies on the road to Ciudad del Este

From Trinidad the road goes through or near a number of German colonies including **Hohenau** (Km 36, www.hohenau.gov.py) and **Parque Manantial** ① *Km 35, 500 m from main road*. The park is in a beautiful location and has two pools (open 0830-2200), a good restaurant, bar, very nice camping ground and complete facilities (US$6.25 per day including use of a swimming pool and all facilities), horse riding, tour of the countryside by jeep and cross country tours to the nearby Jesuit ruins. It's a good place to stop off on the way to Ciudad del Este. Major credit cards accepted and local and national phone calls can be made at no extra charge.

The next colony is **Obligado**; it has an ATM in the centre of town. About 5 km further north is **Bella Vista** (Km 42, also has ATM), where it's possible to visit various yerba mate plantations. The most geared up for visitors is **Pajarito** ① *T0767-240240, www.pajarito.com.py*.

South of Asunción listings

For Sleeping and Eating price codes and other relevant information, see pages 9-10.

Sleeping

Paraguarí and around *p53*
$ pp **Estancia Mónica**, Camino a Cerro Corá, near Acahay, Paraguarí, T03771-216394 or 9-8375 6996, info@paraguay-magazin.com. German/Paraguayan run ranch with B&B and full board for maximum 7 people, offers tours as far as Iguazú, German, English, Spanish spoken. Owner Jan Paessler runs http://wochenblatt.cc, German language newspaper.

Ybycuí *p54*
$ Hotel Pytu'u Renda, Av General Caballero 509 y Quyquyho, T0534-226364. Good food, cooking facilities.
Tourism farm B Estancia Santa Clara, Km 141, Ruta 1, Caapucú, T021-605729, www.estanciasantaclara.com.py. Rural activites in a beautiful setting between Paraguarí and San Ignacio Guazú, full board or visit for the day (mini-zoo). Reserve in advance.

San Ignacio Guazú and around *p54*
$$ Parador Altamirano-Piringó, Ruta 1, Km 224, T082-232334. Modern, on outskirts, with a/c, (**$** pp without), recommended, 24-hr restaurant.
$ pp **Hotel Rural, San Ignacio Country Club**, Ruta 1, Km 230, T082-232895, www.sanignaciocountryclub.com. With full board and Wi-Fi in cabins. Also has shaded camping, US$6 pp, without tent or meals, but other services included, hot water, electricity, tennis, swimming pool, ping pong table, pool, impressive place and very helpful owner, Gustavo Jhave.
$ La Casa de Loly, Mcal López 1595, San Ignacio, T082-232362, http://lacasadeloli.com.py, on outskirts. Nice atmosphere, pool, a/c, with breakfast, other meals on request.

Ayolas, Santiago and San Cosme *p55*
$ Hotel Nacional de Ayolas, Av Costanera, Villa Permanente, T072-222273, www.ayolas.com.py. Overlooking the river, popular with fishing groups.

Encarnación p55, map p56
$$$-$$ Encarnación Resort Hotel,
Villa Quiteria, on outskirts, Ruta 1, Km 361,
T207250, www.encarnacionresorthotel.
com.py. First class, comfortable, very well
run. Highly recommended.
$$ Acuario, J L Mallorquín 1550 y Villarrica,
T202676, www.acuario.com.py. Pool, a/c,
with breakfast.
$$ De La Costa, Av Rodríguez de
Francia 1240 con Cerro Corá, T205694,
www.delacostahotel.com.py. Smart
new hotel, pool, garden, Wi-Fi, parking,
restaurant, breakfast included.
$$-$ Cristal, Mcal Estigarribia 1157 y
Cerro Corá, T202371, cristalh@telesurf.
com.py. Pool, restaurant, TV and a/c,
helpful staff.
$ Central, Mcal López 542 y C A López,
Zona Baja, T203454. With breakfast, nice
patio, German spoken.
$ Germano, General Cabañas y C A
López, opposite bus terminal, T203346.
Cheaper without bath or a/c, German
and Japanese spoken, small, very
accommodating. Highly recommended.
$ Itapúa, C A López y General Cabañas,
T205045, opposite bus station.
Dark rooms, modern.
$ Liz, Av Independencia 1746, T202609.
Comfortable, restaurant, recommended.
$ Paraná, Estigarribia 1414 y Tomas R Pereira
y Villarrica, T204440. Good breakfast, helpful.
Recommended.
$ Viena, PJ Caballero 568, T205981, beside
Copaco. With breakfast, German-run, good
food, garage.

**Santísima Trinidad del Paraná and
Jesús de Tavarangüé** p56
$ pp Hotel a las Ruinas, a good hotel and
restaurant next to the entrance to the hilltop
site of the Jesuit reducción at Trinidad,
T9-8582 8563, a.weisbach@gmx.net.
German-owned, helpful, pool, nice garden.

**German colonies on the road
to Ciuidad del Este** p57
$$$ Biorevital Hotel and Spa, Av Mcal
López 275 y Itapúa (Km 38½), Obligado,
T0717-20073, www.spa-kur.com.py.
German run, includes organic meals,
mineral water pools, sauna, mud baths,
yoga, internet, homeopathic treatments
and various packages offered.
$$ Papillón, Ruta 6, Km 45, Bella Vista,
T0767-240235, www.papillon.com.py.
A/c, internet, pool, gardens, very pleasant,
German, French, English, Flemish spoken,
excellent and popular restaurant, full and
half-board available. Highly recommended.
Organizes excursions in the area including
in a light aircraft.
$ Plaza, Samaniego 1415,
Bella Vista, T0757-240236.

Eating

Paraguarí and around p53
La Frutería, about 2.5 km before the town.
Wide selection of fruit, outdoor seating and
a restaurant serving *empanadas*, hamburgers,
beer, fruit salad. Highly recommended.

Encarnación p55, map p56
$$ American Grill, Av Irrazábal just before
International Bridge. Good *churrasquería*.
$$ Parrillada las Delicias, Mcal Estigarribia
1694. Good steaks, comfortable, Chilean wines.
$$ Provenza, Dr Mallorquín, just past the
rail tracks. International cuisine.
$$ Tokio, Mcal Estigarribia 472. Good
Japanese, real coffee.
$$-$ Cuarajhy, Mcal Estigarribia y Pereira.
Terrace seating, good food, open 24 hrs.
$$-$ Hiroshima, 25 de Mayo y L
Valentinas (no sign), T206288. Excellent
Japanese, wide variety, fresh sushi,
Tue-Sun 1130-1400, 1900-2330.
$ Rubi, Mcal Estigarribia 519. Chinese, good.

Transport

Yaguarón *p53*
Bus Every 15 mins from **Asunción**, US$0.60.

Paraguarí and around *p53*
Bus City buses leave from lower level of the Asunción terminal every 15 mins throughout the day, but much faster to take an Encarnación-bound bus from the upper level, same fare US$0.90.

Parque Nacional Ybycuí *p54*
Bus There are 2 per day, 1000 and 1600 from **Ybycuí**, US$0.60, take bus going to the Mbocaya Pucú colony that stops in front of the park entrance. From Asunción take a bus to Acahay, **Transportes Emilio Cabrera**, 8 daily and change, or bus to Ybycuí, 0630, US$1.30.

San Ignacio Guazú *p54*
Bus Regular services to/from **Asunción**, US$4.30 *común*, US$6.80 *rápido*; to **Encarnación**, frequent, US$5.25 *común*, US$7.80 *rápido*.

Santa María
Bus From **San Ignacio** from the Esso station, 6 a day from 0500, 45 mins.

San Cosme y Damián
Bus From **Encarnación**, La Cosmeña and **Perla del Sur**, US$2.70, 2½ hrs.

Encarnación *p55, map p56*
Bus The bus terminal is at Mcal Estigarribia y Memmel. Good cheap snacks.
To/from **Asunción**, Alborada (T203113, www.excursiones.com.py), La Encarnacena (recommended, T203448, www.laencarnacena.com.py), **Flecha de Oro** (T203970), **Rysa**, at least 4 a day each, 6 hrs, US$12. Stopping (*común*) buses are US$9.50, but much slower (6-7 hrs). To **Ciudad del Este**, US$5.75, several daily, 4 hrs.

Border with Argentina *p56*
Bus Take any 'Posadas/Argentina' bus from opposite bus terminal over the bridge, US$0.65, 30 mins. Keep all luggage with you and retain bus ticket; buses do not wait. After formalities (queues common), use ticket on next bus. **Taxi** costs US$6.75 (at least). **Cycles** are not allowed to use the bridge, but officials may give cyclists a lift. **Ferry** costs US$1.25. Immigration formalities must be undertaken at the main offices.

Santísima Trinidad del Paraná and Jesús de Tavarangüé *p56*
Bus Many go from **Encarnación** to and through Trinidad, take any bus from the terminal marked Hohenau or Ciudad del Este, US$1.25 (beware overcharging). A **taxi** tour from Encarnación costs about US$25. Bus direct **Encarnación-Jesús** 0800; buses run **Jesús-Trinidad** every hr (30 mins, US$0.55), from where it is easy to get back to Encarnación, so do Jesús first. Last bus Jesús-Trinidad 1700; also collective taxis, return Trinidad-Jesús US$3.65. No buses on Sun. Enquire locally as taxis may overcharge.

Directory

Encarnación *p55, map p56*
Banks Most banks now in the upper town, eg **Banco Continental**, Mcal Estigarribia 1418, Visa accepted. **Citibank**, Mcal Estigarribia y Villarrica, ATM. Casas de cambio for cash on Mcal Estagarribia (eg **Cambios Financiero** at No 307, **Cambio Iguazú** at No 211). **Cambio Chaco Irrazábal y Memmel**, inside Superseis supermarket. Moneychangers at the Paraguayan side of the bridge but best to change money in town. **Consulates Argentina**, Artigas 960, T201066, www.consargenc.org.py, Mon-Fri 0800-1300. **Brazil**, Memmel 452, T206335, epgbrvc@itacom.com.py. **Germany**, Jorge Memmel 631, T204041, con_alemana@itacom.com.py. **Telephones** Copaco, Capitán PJ Caballero y Mcal López, 0700-2200, only Spanish spoken.

North of Asunción

The winding Río Paraguay is 400 m wide and is still the main trade route for the products of northern Paraguay, in spite of a paved highway built to Concepción. Boats carry cattle, hides, yerba mate, tobacco and timber. On the river, a boat trip to Concepción is probably one of the most interesting ways to see the countryside and wildlife.

Asunción to Concepción

Travelling north from Asunción by river, you first come across Puente Remanso, the bridge that marks the beginning of the Trans-Chaco Highway. Just further upstream is Villa Hayes, founded in 1786 but renamed in 1879 after the US president who arbitrated the territorial dispute with Argentina in Paraguay's favour. Further upstream is Puerto Antequera and 100 km beyond is Concepción. By road there are two alternative routes. One is via the Trans-Chaco Highway and Pozo Colorado. The Pozo Colorado-Concepción road, 146 km, is completely paved and offers spectacular views of birdlife. The other route is Ruta 2 to Coronel Oviedo, Ruta 3 to Yby Yaú (paved) and then west along Ruta 5 (paved). North of Coronel Oviedo, at Tacuara (Km 225), a road heads west to Rosario, from where you can visit the Mennonite community of **Colonia Volendam**, nine hours by bus from Asunción (two a day, San Jorge, US$3.30). German and Spanish are spoken here.

Concepción → *Phone code: 0331. Population: 76,378.*

Concepción, 312 km north of Asunción, stands on the east bank of the Río Paraguay. It is known as La Perla del Norte for its climate and setting. To appreciate the colonial aspect of the city, walk away from the main commercial streets. At Plaza La Libertad are the Catedral and recently restored Municipalidad. Sunsets from the port are beautiful. The town is the trade centre of the north, doing a considerable business with Brazil. The **Brazilian Consulate** ⓘ *Pdte Franco 972, T342655, Mon-Fri 0800-1400, brvcconcep@tigo.com.py*, issues visas, but go early to ensure same-day processing. The market, a good place to try local food, is east of the main street, Agustín Pinedo (which is a kind of open-air museum). From here Avenida Presidente Franco runs west to the port. Along Avenida Agustín Pineda is a large statue of María Auxiliadora with Christ child. There are stairs to balconies at the base of the monument which offer good views of the city. The **Museo Municipal** ⓘ *Mcal López y Cerro Corá, Mon-Fri 0700-1200*, contains a collection of guns, religious and other objects. Plaza Agustín Fernando de Pinedo has a permanent craft market. About 9 km south is a bridge across the Río Paraguay, which makes for an interesting walk across the shallows and islands to the west bank and the Chaco, about an hour return trip, taxi US$6. The island in the Río Paraguay facing Concepción is Isla Chaco'i, soon to be a free trade zone but at present largely empty, where you can stroll through the fields. Row boats take passengers to the island from the shore next to the port, US$0.25 per person. For more information visit the town's own blog, http://concepcionparaguay.blogspot.com.

East of Concepción

There is a 215-km road (Ruta 5 – fully paved) from Concepción, eastwards to the Brazilian border. This road goes through Horqueta, Km 50, a fast-growing cattle and lumber town of 55,882 people. Further on the road is very scenic. From **Yby Yaú** (junction with Ruta 8 south to Coronel Oviedo) the road continues to Pedro Juan Caballero.

Six kilometres east of Yby Yaú a road branches off to the pleasant **Parque Nacional Cerro Corá** (12,038 ha, www.salvemoslos.com.py/pncc.htm), the site of Mariscal Francisco Solano López' death and the final defeat of Paraguay in the War of the Triple Alliance. There is a monument to him and other national heroes; the site is constantly guarded. It has hills and cliffs (some with pre-Columbian caves and petroglyphs), camping facilities, swimming and hiking trails. The rocky outcrops are spectacular and the warden is helpful and provides free guides. When you have walked up the road and seen the line of leaders' heads, turn right and go up the track passing a dirty-looking shack (straight on leads to a military base). Administration office is 5 km east of the main entrance at Km 180 on Ruta 5.

Pedro Juan Caballero → *Phone code: 0336. Population: 75,109.*

This border town is separated from the Brazilian town of Ponta Porã, by a road (Dr Francia on the Paraguayan side, on the Brazilian side either Rua Marechal Floreano or Avenida Internacional): which anyone can cross at their leisure (see below for immigration formalities). Ponta Porã is the more modern and prosperous of the two. In addition to liquor and electronics, everything costs less on the Paraguayan side. **Shopping China** is a vast emporium on the eastern outskirts of town and **Maxi** is a large well stocked supermarket in the centre. You can pay in guaraníes, reais or US$, at good exchange rates. **Arte Paraguaya**, Mcal López y Alberdi, has a good selection of crafts from all over the country.

Border with Brazil

This is a more relaxed crossing than Ciudad del Este and generally much faster. For day crossings you do not need a stamp, but passports must be stamped if travelling beyond the border towns (ask if unsure whether your destination is considered beyond). **Paraguayan immigration** ⓘ *T0336-272195, Mon-Fri 0700-2100, Sat 0800-2100, Sun 1900-2100, take bus line 2 on the Paraguayan side, or any Brazilian city bus that goes to the Rodoviária, taxi US$4.50*, is in the customs building on the eastern outskirts of town near *Shopping China*. Then report to Brazilian federal police in Ponta Porã (closed Sat-Sun). The **Brazilian consulate** ⓘ *Mcal Estigarribia 250, T0336-273562, Mon-Fri 0800-1300*, issues visas, fees payable only in guaraníes, take passport and a photo, go early to get visa the same day. There is another crossing to Brazil at Bella Vista on the Río Apá, northwest of PJ Caballero; buses run from the Brazilian border town of Bela Vista to Jardim and on to Campo Grande. There is a Paraguayan immigration office at Bella Vista, but no Brazilian Policia Federal in Bela Vista. To cross here, get Paraguayan exit stamp then report to the local Brazilian police who may give a temporary stamp, but you must later go to the Policia Federal in either Ponta Porã or Corumbá. Do not fail to get the proper stamp later or you will be detained upon re-entering Paraguay.

North of Asunción listings

For Sleeping and Eating price codes and other relevant information, see pages 9-10.

Sleeping

Asunción to Concepción p60

$$ pp Estancia Jejui, set on the Río Jejui, 65 km north of Tacuara on Ruta 3, address in Asunción, Telmo Aquino 4068, T021-600227, www.coinco.com.py/jejui. All rooms with a/c, bathroom and hot water, fishing, horse riding, tennis, boat rides extra, US$62 pp including all meals.

$ pp Hotel Waldbrunner, Colonia Volendam, T0451-20175, www.hotel-waldbrunner.de. Bath, **$** without a/c, also has a good restaurant.

Concepción p60

$$ Concepción Palace, Mcal López 399 esq E A Garay, T241858, www.concepcionpalace.com.py. By far the nicest hotel in town. New and with all mod cons, pool, a/c, restaurant, Wi-Fi throughout, large rooms.

$$ Francés, Franco y C A López, T242750, www.hotelfrancesconcepcion.com. With a/c, **$** with fan, breakfast, rooms are ageing, nice grounds with pool (US$1 non-guests), restaurant, parking.

$$ Victoria, Franco y PJ Caballero 693, T242256. Pleasant rooms, a/c, fridge, **$** with fan, restaurant, parking.

$ Concepción, Don Bosco y Cabral near market, T242360. With simple breakfast, a/c, cheaper with fan, family run, good value.

Pedro Juan Caballero p61

$$$ Casino Amambay, Av Dr Francia 1 y José Bergés at the west end of town, T271140, www.casinocity.com/py. A posh establishment centred around its casino, simple rooms compared to its surroundings, include buffet breakfast, a/c, fridge, balcony, lovely grounds with large pool. Noisy and crowded on weekends and holidays.

$$ Eiruzú, Mcal López y Mcal Estigarribia, T272435, http://hoteleiruzu.blogspot.com. With breakfast, a/c, fridge and pool, starting to show its age but still good.

$$ Porã Palace, Alberdi 30 y Dr Francia, T273022, www.porapalacehotel.com. With breakfast, a/c, fridge, balcony, restaurant, pool, aging but still OK, rooms in upper floor have been refurbished and are nicer.

$ Victoria, Teniente Herrero y Alberdi, near bus station, T272733. With breakfast, electric shower and a/c, cheaper with fan, family run, simple. Cheapest decent lodgings in town.

Eating

Concepción p60

$ Hotel Francés, good value buffet lunch, à la carte in the evening.

$ Hotel Victoria, set lunches and à la carte, grill in *quincho* across the street.

$ Pollería El Bigote, Pdte Franco y E A Garay. Simple, good chicken, sidewalk seating.

$ Ysapy, Yegros y Mcal Estigarribia at Plaza Pineda. Pizza and ice-cream, terrace or sidewalk seating, very popular, daily 1630-0200.

Pedro Juan Caballero p61

$ Mr Grill at *Maxi* supermarket, Mcal López y J Estigarribia. Good quality buffet by the kilo.

$ Pepes, Dr Francia y Alberdi. Buffet, à la carte.

$ Pizza House, Mcal López y José de J Martínez.

Transport

Concepción p60

Bus The terminal is on the outskirts, 8 blocks north along General Garay, but buses also stop in the centre, Av Pinedo, look for signs Parada Omnibus. A shuttle bus (Línea 1) runs between the terminal and the port. Taxi from terminal or port to centre, US$2.50; terminal to port U$3.25. To **Asunción**, 7 a day with

N S de Asunción/Golondrina, 2 with Santaniana (www.lasantaniana.com.py), plus other companies, US$13, 5½ hrs via Pozo Colorado, 9 hrs via Coronel Oviedo. To **Pedro Juan Caballero**, frequent service, several companies, US$4.75, 4-5 hrs. To **Horqueta**, 1 hr, US$1.10. To **Filadelfia**, N S de Asunción/Golondrina direct at 0730 daily, US$12, 5 hrs, otherwise change at Pozo Colorado. To **Ciudad del Este**, García direct at 1230 daily, US$13, 9 hrs, or change at Coronel Oviedo.

Boat To **Asunción**, the Cacique II sails Mon between 0600 and 0700 (if enough passengers), 22-24 hrs, tickets sold on board in advance of departure (fares and other services on page 27). To **Fuerte Olimpo**, **Bahía Negra**, and intermediate points along the upper Río Paraguay, the **Río Aquidabán** sails Tue 1100, arriving Bahía Negra on Fri morning and returning immediately to arrive back in Concepción on Sun, US$19 to Bahía Negra plus US$9 for a berth if you want one. Take food and water. Tickets sold in office just outside the port, T242435, Mon-Sat 0700-1200. There are sporadic ferries from Concepción to Isla Margarita, across from Porto Murtinho, Brazil. Ask for prices and times at dock and note that service does not include anything other than standing room. Motorboats (*deslizadores*) may be hired but beware overcharging and seek advice from the Prefectura Naval.
Note There is an immigration office in Concepción (see below), but not further towards Brazil. Check well in advance, even in Asunción, about obtaining an exit stamp in good time. In all, a time consuming, adventurous and expensive journey.

Pedro Juan Caballero *p61*
Bus To **Concepción**, frequent, 4-5 hrs, US$4.75. To **Asunción**, 5-6 hrs via 25 de Diciembre, 7½ hrs via Coronel Oviedo. Santaniana has nicest buses, *bus cama* US$13.35; *semicama* US$11.10. **Amambay** 0700 via Oviedo US$11.10, twice via 25 de Diciembre, US$11.75. **N S de Asunción** 2 a day US$11.10. To **Bella Vista**, Perpetuo Socorro 3 a day, US$4.50, 4 hrs. To **Campo Grande** Amambay 3 a day, US$13.75, 5 hrs, they stop at Policia Federal in Ponta Porã for entry stamp.

Directory

Concepción *p60*
Banks TCs cannot be changed. **Norte Cambios**, Pdte Franco y 14 de Mayo, Mon-Fri 0830-1700, Sat 0830-1100, fair rates for US$ and euros, cash only. **Financiera Familiar**, Pdte Franco y General Garay, US$ cash only. **Immigration** Registro Civil, Pdte Franco y Caballero, T9-7219 3143. **Internet** Cybercom Internet Café, Pdte Franco y 14 de Mayo, open until 2230. **Post office** Pdte Franco. **Telephone** Copaco and other cabinas on Pdte Franco.

Pedro Juan Caballero *p61*
Banks Many *cambios* on the Paraguayan side, especially on Curupayty between Dr Francia and Mcal López. Good rates for buying guaraníes or reais with US$ or euros cash, better than inside Brazil, but TCs are usually impossible to change and there is only one ATM. Banks on Brazilian side do not change cash or TCs but have a variety of ATMs. **BBVA**, Dr Francia y Mcal Estigarribia. Mon-Fri 0845-1300, changes US$ cash to guaraníes only, and has Cirrus ATM. **Norte Cambios**, Curupayty entre Dr Francia y Mcal López, Mon-Fri 0830-1630, Sat 0830-1100, fair rates for cash, 5% commission for TCs. **Internet** Several places including **Maxi supermarket**, spacious, quiet, a/c, US$1 per hr. **Telephones** Copaco, behind the bus station, plus many *cabinas*.

The Chaco

West of the Río Paraguay is the Chaco, a wild expanse of palm savanna and marshes (known as Humid, or Bajo Chaco, closest to the Río Paraguay) and dry scrub forest and farmland (known as Dry, or Alto Chaco, further northwest from the river). The Chaco has a substantial population of indigenous peoples. Birdlife is spectacular and abundant. Large cattle estancias dot the whole region, but otherwise agriculture has been developed mainly by German-speaking Mennonites from Russia in the Chaco Central. Through this vast area the Trans-Chaco Highway (Ruta 9) runs to Bolivia. Most of the region is pristine, perfect for those who want to escape into the wilderness with minimal human contact and experience nature at its finest. Although the government has made much of its interest in promoting tourism in the Chaco, it is also considerably lacking in infrastructure, so travellers should prepare accordingly.

Ins and outs
Getting there The Paraguayan Chaco covers over 24 million ha, but once away from the vicinity of Asunción, the average density is far less than one person to the sq km. A single major highway, the Ruta Trans-Chaco, runs in an almost straight line northwest towards the Bolivian border, ostensibly forming part of the *corredor bi-oceánico*, connecting ports on the Pacific and Atlantic oceans, although it has yet to live up to its expectations. The elevation rises very gradually from 50 m opposite Asunción to 450 m on the Bolivian border. Paving of the Trans-Chaco to the Bolivian border (Infante Rivarola) was completed in 2007. However, in spite of being graded twice a year, several sections paved earlier, such as La Patria to Mariscal Estigarribia (the first Paraguayan immigration post coming from Bolivia) are already showing signs of wear and tear, with repairs to potholes few and far between. Sand berms also form at will in some sections and must be avoided. From the border to Villamontes, the road is gravel and in good condition even after rain, and a 4WD is no longer indispensable. The first 55 km out of Villamontes are paved, and the remainder is in progress. Although road conditions are much improved, motorists and even travellers going by bus should carry extra food and especially water; climatic conditions are harsh and there is little traffic in case of a breakdown. ▸▸ *See also Transport, page 70.*

Getting around Most bus companies have some a/c buses on their Chaco routes (a great asset December-March), enquire in advance. There is very little local public transport between the main Mennonite towns, you must use the buses heading to/from Asunción to travel between them as well as Mariscal Estigarribia. No private expedition should leave the

Trans-Chaco without plentiful supplies of water, food and fuel. No one should venture onto the dirt roads alone and since this is a major smuggling route from Bolivia, it is unwise to stop for anyone at night. There are service stations at regular intervals along the highway in the Bajo and Chaco Central, but beyond Mariscal Estigarribia there is one stop for diesel only and no regular petrol at all until Villamontes, a long drive. Winter temperatures are warm by day, cooler by night, but summer heat and mosquitoes can make it very unpleasant (pyrethrum coils, *espirales*, are sold everywhere). Any unusual insect bites should be examined immediately upon arrival, as Chagas disease is endemic in the Chaco.

Information Consejo Regional de Turismo Chaco Central (CONRETUR) coordinates tourism development of the three cooperatives and the private sector. Contact **Hans Fast** ⓘ *T492-52422, Loma Plata, fast@telesurf.com.py*. The **Fundación para el Desarrollo Sustentable del Chaco** ⓘ *Deportivo 935 y Algarrobo, Loma Plata, T492-52235, www.desdelchaco.org.py*, operates conservation projects in the area and has useful information but does not offer tours. ▸▸ *For Tour operators, see page 70. Always examine in detail a tour operator's claims to expertise int he Chaco. See also under individual towns for local tourist offices.*

Background
The Bajo Chaco begins on the riverbank just west of Asunción across the Río Paraguay. It is a picturesque landscape of palm savanna, much of which is seasonally inundated because of the impenetrable clay beneath the surface, although there are 'islands' of higher ground with forest vegetation. Cattle ranching on huge estancias is the prevailing economic activity; some units lie several hundred kilometres down tracks off the highway. Remote estancias have their own airfields, and all are equipped with two-way radios. Never wander into one unless you have prior permission from the owner, except in an emergency. There have been cases of guards shooting travellers mistaken for smugglers.

In the **Chaco Central**, the natural vegetation is dry scrub forest, with a mixture of hardwoods and cactus. The *palo borracho* (bottle tree) with its pear-shaped, water-conserving, trunk, the *palo santo*, with its green wood and beautiful scent, and the tannin-rich *quebracho* (literally meaning axe-breaker) are the most noteworthy native species. This is the best area in Paraguay to see large mammals, especially once away from the central Chaco Mennonite colonies.

The **Alto Chaco** is characterized by low dense thorn and scrub forest which has created an impenetrable barricade of spikes and spiny branches resistant to heat and drought and very tough on tyres. Towards Bolivia cacti become more prevalent as rainfall decreases. There are a few estancias in the southern part, but beyond Mariscal Estigarribia there are no towns, only occasional military checkpoints. Summer temperatures often exceed 45°C.

Reserva de la Biosfera del Chaco
This is the crown jewel of Paraguay's national park system, albeit one without infrastructure and nearly impossible to visit. **Guyra Paraguay**, which currently co-manages the national parks in this region, is possibly the best option for arranging a tour (see page 7 and Activities and tours, below). Note that any expedition to the Reserve

will be a very costly undertaking and must be cleared with government authorities well ahead of time. The 4.7-million-ha biosphere reserve in the Chaco and Pantanal eco-systems is a UNESCO Man and Biosphere Reserve and includes four national parks: Defensores del Chaco, Médanos del Chaco, Teniente Agripino Enciso and Río Negro; the Cerro Chovoreca monument; and the Cerro Cabrera-Timané reserve. All are north of the Trans-Chaco and most are along the Bolivian border. Teniente Enciso, the smallest park, is currently the only one accessible by public transport, although not easily, see below. The others can only be visited with a private 4WD vehicle, or on expensive tours from Loma Plata and Asunción. Most of Paraguay's few remaining jaguars are found here. Puma, tapir and peccary also inhabit the area, as well as taguá (an endemic peccary) and a short-haired guanaco. The best time to see them is around waterholes at nightfall in the dry season, but with great patience. **Cerro León** (highest peak 600 m), one of the only hilly areas of the Chaco, is located within this reserve. Roads from Filadelfia through this area are very rough, for 4WDs and during the dry season only. Information in Spanish at www.elgranchaco.com.

Parque Nacional Defensores del Chaco (www.salvemoslos.com.py/pdchaco.htm), recently declared as having an environment of "maximum value" by both the World Bank and the Paraguayan government, is considered a pristine environment and the gateway to the seventh-largest ecosystem in Latin America. It is some 220 km from Filadelfia, has three visitor centres with rustic accommodation, a/c, kitchen and shared bathroom. Distances between sites are long. **Parque Nacional Teniente Agripino Enciso** (www.salvemoslos.com.py/pntae.htm), 20 km from La Patria, has a good visitor centre with accommodation, one room with bathroom, others shared, a/c, take sleeping bag and all food. **N S de Asunción** minibuses run from Filadelfia to Teniente Enciso via Mariscal Estigarribia and La Patria, see Transport, page 70.

The Trans-Chaco Highway

To reach the Ruta Trans-Chaco, leave Asunción behind and cross the Río Paraguay to Villa Hayes. Birdlife is immediately more abundant and easily visible in the palm savanna (binoculars and camera highly recommended), but other wildlife is usually only seen at night, and otherwise occurs mostly as road kills. The first service station after Asunción is at Km 130. **Pirahú**, Km 252, has a service station and is a good place to stop for a meal; it has a/c, delicious empanadas and fruit salad. The owner of the **Ka-Í** parador owns an old-fashioned carbon manufacturing site 2 km before Pirahú. Ask for him if you are interested in visiting the site. At Km 271 is **Pozo Colorado** and the turning for Concepción (see page 60). There are two restaurants, a basic hotel (**$** pp with fan, cheaper without), supermarket, hospital, a service station and a military post. The Touring y Automóvil Club Paraguayo provides a breakdown and recovery service from Pozo Colorado (T9-8193 9611, www.tacpy.com.py). At this point, the tidy Mennonite homesteads, with flower gardens and citrus orchards, begin to appear. At Km 282, 14 km northwest of Pozo Colorado, is **Rancho Buffalo Bill**, T021-298381, one of the most pleasant places to stop off or eat, beside a small lake. The estancia has limited but good accommodation (**$**), ask at restaurant. Horse riding, nature walks and camping are good options here. At Km 320 is **Río Verde**, with fuel, police station and restaurant. The next good place to stay or eat along the Trans-Chaco is **Cruce de los Pioneros**, at Km 415, where accommodation (**$** Los Pioneros, T491-432170, hot shower, a/c), limited supermarket, vehicle repair shop, and fuel are available. A new paved road has been built from Cruce Boquerón, just northwest of Cruce de los Pioneros, to Loma Plata. In mid-September the country's biggest motorsport event, the Trans-Chaco Rally (www.transchacorally.com.py), is held.

Mennonite communities
The Chaco Central has been settled by Mennonites, Anabaptists of German extraction who began arriving in the late 1920s. There are three administratively distinct but adjacent colonies: Menno (from Russia via Canada); Fernheim (directly from Russia) and Neuland (the last group to arrive, also from Russia, after the Second World War). Among themselves, the Mennonites speak 'plattdeutsch' ('Low German'), but they readily speak and understand 'hochdeutsch' ('High German'), which is the language of instruction in their schools. Increasingly, younger Mennonites speak Spanish and some English. The people are friendly and willing to talk about their history and culture. Altogether there are about 80 villages with a population of about 18,000 Mennonites and 20,000 *indígenas*. Increasing numbers of Paraguayans are migrating to the area in search of economic opportunities while indigenous people (eight distinct groups) occupy the lowest rung on the socioeconomic ladder.

The Mennonites have created a remarkable oasis of regimented prosperity in this harsh hinterland. Their hotels and restaurants are impeccably clean, services are very efficient, large modern supermarkets are well stocked with excellent dairy products and all other goods, local and imported. Each colony has its own interesting museum. All services, except for hotels, a few restaurants and one gas station in Filadelfia, close on Saturday afternoon and Sunday. The main towns are all very spread out and have no public transport except for a few expensive taxis in Filadelfia, most residents use their private vehicles. Walking around in the dust and extreme heat can be tiring. Transport between the three main towns is also limited, see Transport, page 70.

Filadelfia → *Phone code: 0491. Population: 9713.*
Also known as Fernheim Colony, Filadelfia, 466 km from Asunción, is the largest town of the region. The **Jacob Unger Museum** ① *C Hindenburg y Unruh, T32151, US$1 including video*, provides a glimpse of pioneer life in the Chaco, as well as exhibiting artefacts of the indigenous peoples of the region. The manager of the Hotel Florida will open the museum upon request, mornings only. Next to the museum is **Plaza de los Recuerdos**, a good place to see the *samu'u* or *palo borracho* (bottle tree). A bookstore-cum-craft shop, **Librería El Mensajero**, next to Hotel Florida, is run by Sra Penner, very helpful and informative.

The Fernheim community does not encourage tourism, but there is a website, www.filadelfiaparaguay.com. Apart from that, there is no tourist infrastructure in Filadelfia. General information may be obtained from the co-op office.

Loma Plata → *Phone code: 0492. Population: 4118.*
The centre of Menno Colony, Loma Plata is 25 km east of Filadelfia. Although smaller than Filadelfia, it has more to offer the visitor. It has a good museum **Museo de la Colonia Menno** ① *Mon-Fri 0700-1130, 1400-1800, Sat 0700-1300, US$1.85*. **Balneario Oasis swimming complex** ① *Nord Grenze, 700 m past airport north of Loma Plata, T52704, US$1.85, Sep-Apr 1500-2100, except Sun and holidays, 1100-2100*, has three pools with slides and snack bar, a welcome break from the summer heat. **Tourist office** (contact

Walter Ratzlaff) ⓘ *next to the Chortitzer Komitee Co-op, T492-52301, turismo@ chortitzer.com.py, Mon-Fri 0700-1130, 1400-1800, Sat 0700-1300*, very helpful. For general information about the colony, not tourism, www.chortitzer.com.py.

Wetlands around Loma Plata To the southeast of Loma Plata is the Riacho Yacaré Sur watershed, with many salt water lagoons, generally referred to as Laguna Salada. This is a wonderful place to see waterbirds such as Chilean flamingos, swans, spoonbills and migratory shorebirds from the Arctic. There are extensive walks though the eerily beautiful landscape. **Laguna Capitán**, a 22-ha recreation reserve, 30 km from town, has several small lagoons, a swimming lake, basic bunk bed accommodation (**$** per person, shared bath), kitchen facilities, meals on request, camping (US$1.15 per person). Reserve directly at T9-9165 0101 or through the Cooperative information office in Loma Plata. There is no public transport. Taxi US$24 one way; full-day tour combining Laguna Capitán with visit to the Cooperative's installations and museum, US$67.50 per group plus transport. Guides are required for visits. **Laguna Chaco Lodge** ⓘ *70 km from town, T52235*, a 2500-ha-private reserve, is a Ramsar wetland site (no accommodation). The lovely Laguna Flamenco is the main body of water surrounded by dry forest. Large numbers of Chilean flamingos and other water birds may be seen here. **Campo María**, a 4500-ha reserve owned by the Chortitzer Komitee, but 90 km from town, also has a large lake and can be visited on a tour.

Indigenous Foundation for Agricultural and Livestock Development (FIDA) ⓘ *30 km from Neuland, Filadelfia and Loma Plata, T0491-32116*. Located within Yalve Sanga, this is the first indigenous version of the Mennonite cooperative colonies and provides an interesting insight into the lives of the communities. Limited handicrafts are sold in the Yalve Sanga supermarket (better selection in Neuland).

Neuland → *Phone code: 0493. Population: 1800.*

Neuland, also known as Neu-Halbstadt, is 33 km south of Filadelfia. To the extent that the High Chaco has a tourism infrastructure at all, it is located squarely in Neuland, a well-organized town. There is a small **Museo Histórico** with objects brought by the first Mennonites from Russia, set in the building of the first primary school of the area. **Neuland Beach Park** ⓘ *US$1.75, pool, snack bar with a/c*. Parque la Amistad, 500 m past pool, is 35 ha of natural vegetation where paths have been cleared for nature walks. Most spectacular are the wild orchids (September-October), cacti and birdlife. Enrique (Heinz) Weibe ⓘ *T971-701 634, hwiebe@neuland.com.py* is the official guide of the Neuland colony; also ask for Harry Epp ⓘ *contact through Neuland Co-op office, T0493-240201, www.neuland.com.py, Mon-Fri 0700-1130, 1400-1800, Sat 0700-1130*, who is very knowledgeable about the flora and fauna and is an informative and entertaining guide. He also gives tours of Neuland in a horse drawn carriage. Phone booths and post office are in centre of town next to the supermarket.

Fortín Boquerón, 27 km from Neuland, is the site of the decisive battle of Chaco War (September 1932) and includes a memorial, a small, well-presented museum and walks around the remainder of the trenches. **Campamento Aurora Chaqueña** is a park 15 km from town on the way to Fortín Boquerón, there is simple accommodation with fan (**$** per person, take your own food and water). **Parque Valle Natural**, 10 km from Neuland on the way to Filadelfia, is an *espartillar*, a dry riverbed with natural brush around it and a few larger trees. Camping is possible although there is only a small covered area. All three sites are easily reached from Neuland as part of a package tour.

Mariscal Estigarribia and on to Bolivia → *Population: 11,665.*

Around 525 Km from Asunción, Mariscal Estigarribia is a former garrison town with aspirations of becoming a transport hub. The few services are spread out over four km along the highway: three gas stations (no fuel stations between Mariscal Estigarribia and Villamontes on the Bolivian side), a couple of small supermarkets (La Llave del Chaco is recommended), two mediocre hotels, and one remarkably excellent restaurant (see listings below). Better services are found in Filadelfia, Loma Plata and Neuland. The immigration office (supposedly 24 hours, but often closed in the small hours) is at the southeast end of town near the Shell station. All buses stop at the terminal (**Parador Arami**), at the northwest end of town, where travellers entering from Bolivia are subject to thorough searches for drugs. The people are friendly and helpful. There is good birdwatching nearby along the dirt road called Picada 500, as well as some indigenous communities nearby where crafts are made.

There are no reliable services of any kind beyond Mariscal Estigarribia. At **La Patria**, 125 km northwest, the road divides: 128 km west to Infante Rivarola continuing to Villamontes, Bolivia, with Bolivian immigration and customs at Ibibobo; 128 km northwest to General Eugenio A Garay continuing to Boyuibe, Bolivia (hardly used as shifting sand makes it treacherous). Immigration posts are at Mariscal Estigarribia and Ibibobo (the latter often closed, so always best to use the former). There are customs posts at either side of the actual border in addition to the main customs offices in Mariscal Estigarribia and Villamontes.

In Bolivia, from Villamontes or Boyuibe, a paved road runs north to Santa Cruz and south to Yacuiba on the Argentine border, see page . Take small denomination dollar notes as it is impossible to buy bolivianos before reaching Bolivia (if entering from Bolivia only *casas de cambio* in Santa Cruz or Puerto Suárez have guaraníes).

The Chaco listings

For Sleeping and Eating price codes and other relevant information, see , pages 9-10.

Sleeping

Filadelfia *p67*
$$-$ Golondrina, Av Hindenburg 635-S at entrance to town, T432643, www.hotel golondrina.com. Modern, 4 types of room with breakfast, a/c, TV and fridge in the best (cheapest with fan, shared bath, no breakfast), restaurant.
$ Florida, Av Hindenburg 165-S opposite park, T432152/4, hotelflorida@telesurf.com.py. Breakfast, a/c, fridge, cheaper in basic annex with shared bath, fan and without breakfast. Pool (US$1.50 per hr for non-guests), restaurant (R) for buffet and à la carte.

$ Safari, Industrial 194-E, T432218, www.hotel-safari.com. Modern, clean, spacious common areas with game room. Spanish and German spoken. Same owners as **Golondrina** above.

Loma Plata *p67*
$ Mora, Sandstrasse 803, T252255. With breakfast, a/c, new wing has spacious rooms with fridge, nice grounds, family run, good value, good breakfast, basic meals available on request. Recommended.
$ Palace, Av Fred Engen, T252180, hpalace@telesurf.com.py. With breakfast, TV, a/c, mini bar, decent restaurant set around indoor pool (free for diners), friendly staff, best facilities in town.

$ Pensión Loma Plata, J B Reimer 1805, T452829. A/c, breakfast, comfortable rooms, homely atmosphere, very helpful, good value. Includes breakfast, other meals on request. Recommended.

Neuland p68
$ Hotel Boquerón, Av 1 de Febrero opposite the Cooperative, T0493-240306, cfiss@telesurf.com.py. With breakfast, a/c, cheaper in older wing without TV, restaurant.
$ Parador, Av 1 de Febrero y C Talleres, T0493-240567. With breakfast, a/c, cheaper with fan and shared bath, restaurant.

Mariscal Estigarribia p69
$ Parador Arami, northwest end of town and far from everything, also known as *la terminal*, T0494-247230. Functional rooms, a/c, meals on request, agents for Stel Turismo and N S de Asunción buses.

Eating

Filadelfia p67
$$ El Girasol, Unruh 126-E y Hindenburg. Mon-Sat 1100-1400, 1800-2300, Sun 1100-1400. Good buffet and *rodizio*, cheaper without the meat.

Loma Plata p67
$$ Chaco's Grill, Av Dr Manuel Gondra, T52166. Buffet, *rodizio*, very good, patio, live music.
$ Norteño, opposite supermarket. Good, simple, lunch till 1400 then open for dinner.
$ Pizzería San Marino, Av Central y Dr Gondra. Daily 1800-2300. Pizza and German dishes.

Mariscal Estigarribia p69
$$ Italiano, at the southwest end of town behind the Shell station, T0494-247231. Open daily for lunch and dinner. Excellent, top quality meat, large portions, an unexpected treat in the outback. Italian owner Mauricio is friendly and helpful.

Activities and tours

Many agencies in Asunción offer Chaco tours. Note that some are just a visit to Rancho Buffalo Bill and do not provide a good overview of attractions. Hans Fast and Harry Epp also run tours to national parks. In Loma Plata ask around for bicycle hire to explore nearby villages. For more complete tailor-made tours, contact **Guyra Paraguay** (www.guyra.org.py). This organization at present (2011) does not offer tours of the Chaco, but can arrange them.

Transport

Filadelfia p67
Bus From **Asunción**, N S de Asunción/Golondrina, at least 2 daily; Stel Turismo, 1 overnight; 6-7 hrs, US$14. To **Loma Plata**, N S de Asunción/ Golondrina 0800 going to Asunción, 0600 and 1900 coming from Asunción, 1 hr, US$2.25. To **Neuland**, local service Mon-Fri 1130 and 1800, 1 hr, US$2.25. Also Stel Turismo at 1900 and N S de Asunción/Golondrina at 2130, both coming from Asunción. To **Mariscal Estigarribia**, Ovetense at 1800 coming from Asunción, 1½ hrs, US$2.40. Also N S de Asunción at 0500 Mon and Fri, continuing to La Patria and Parque Nacional Teniente Enciso (see page 66), 5-6 hrs, US$9, returns around 1300 same day (confirm all details in advance).

Loma Plata p67
Bus **Asunción**, N S de Asunción/Golondrina, 0600 daily, 7-8 hrs, US$14. To **Filadelfia**, Mon-Fri 1300, Sat 1100, Sun 1200, daily 2130, all continuing to Asunción, 1 hr, US$2.25.

Neuland p68
Bus To **Asunción**, N S de Asunción/Golondrina at 1945, and Stel Turismo at 1800, via Filadelfia, 7-8 hrs, US$14. Local service to Filadelfia, Mon-Fri 0500, 1230, 1 hr, US$2.25.

Mariscal Estigarribia p69
Bus From **Filadelfia** Nasa/Golondrina 1100 daily, **Ovetense** 1200 and 2000 daily; **Asunción** Nasa/Golondrina, daily 1430; **Stel**, 2 a day, and **Pycasu** 3 daily, 7-8 hrs, US$14, 0700. Buses from Asunción pass through town around 0300-0400 en route to Bolivia: **Yaciretá** on Tue, Thu, Sat, Sun (agent at Barcos y Rodados petrol station, T0494-247320); **Stel Turismo** daily (agent at Parador Arami, T0494-247230). You can book and purchase seats in advance but beware overcharging, the fare from Mariscal Estigarribia should be about US$10 less than from Asunción.

Directory

Filadelfia p67
Banks There are no ATMs in the Chaco, neither in the Mennonite colonies nor in Mariscal Estigarribia. **Fernheim Cooperative Bank**, Hindenburg opposite the Cooperative building, changes US$ and euro cash, no commission for US$ TCs (although must be from major issuer). **Internet** At Shopping Portal del Chaco and opposite **Radio ZP30**.
Telephone **Copaco** on Hindenburg, opposite supermarket, Mon-Sat 0700-2100, Sun 0700-1200, 1500-2000.

Loma Plata p67
Banks Chortitzer Komitee Co-op, Av Central, Mon-Fri 0700-1730, Sat 0700-1100, good rates for US$ and euros, US$1.25 commission per TC.
Internet Microtec, Fred Engen 1229, Mon-Sat 0800-1130, 1400-2200, US$0.80 per hr. **Telephone** Copaco, Av Central near supermarket, Mon-Sat 0700-2000, Sun 0700-1200, 1500-2000.

Neuland p68
Banks Neuland Cooperative changes US$ cash and TCs, Mon-Fri 0700-1130, 1400-1800, Sat 0700-1130.

Mariscal Estigarribia p69
Banks No banks. Shell station best for US$, cash only. **Telephones** Copaco, 1 street back from highway, ask for directions.

Footnotes

Contents

74 Index

Index

A
accommodation 9
Areguá 31
Asunción 14

C
Caacupé 32
Capiatá 31
Capitán Badó 33
Carapeguá 54
Cerro Corá 61
Chaco 64
Chololó 54
Ciudad del Este 34
climate 8
Colonia Independencia 34
Colonia Volendam 60
Concepción 60
Coronel Oviedo 33

D
drink 10

E
Encarnación 55

F
Filadelfia 67
food and drink 9
Foz do Iguaçu 48

G
Guaíra 52

H
Hernandarias 35
Hohenau 57
holidays and festivals 11

I
Iguazú Falls 40
Itá 53
Itaipú 35
Itaipu Dam 48
Itauguá 31
itineraries 6

J
Jesús de Tavarangüé 56

L
Lago Ypacaraí 32
Loma Plata 67
Luque 18

M
Mariscal Estigarribia 69
Mbaracayú Forest Reserve 33
Mbutuy 33
money 11

N
Neu-Halbstadt 68
Neuland 68
Nueva Germania 33

P
Paraguarí 53
Parque Manantial 57
Parque Nacional Iguazú 41
Pedro Juan Caballero 61
Piribebuy 32
Pozo Colorado 66
Puerto Iguazú 42

R
Reserva de la Biósfera del Chaco 65

S
safety 11
Salto del Guaíra 33
San Bernardino 32
San Ignacio Guazú 54
San Lorenzo 17
Santa María 54
Santa Rosa 55

T
Tobati 32
tourist information 12
transport, air 9
Trinidad 56

V
Villa Florida 54
Villarrica 33

Y
Yaguarón 53
Ybycuí 54

Titles available in the Footprint *Focus* range

Latin America	UK RRP	US RRP
Bahia & Salvador	£7.99	$11.95
Buenos Aires & Pampas	£7.99	$11.95
Costa Rica	£8.99	$12.95
Cuzco, La Paz & Lake Titicaca	£8.99	$12.95
El Salvador	£5.99	$8.95
Guadalajara & Pacific Coast	£6.99	$9.95
Guatemala	£8.99	$12.95
Guyana, Guyane & Suriname	£5.99	$8.95
Havana	£6.99	$9.95
Honduras	£7.99	$11.95
Nicaragua	£7.99	$11.95
Paraguay	£5.99	$8.95
Quito & Galápagos Islands	£7.99	$11.95
Recife & Northeast Brazil	£7.99	$11.95
Rio de Janeiro	£8.99	$12.95
São Paulo	£5.99	$8.95
Uruguay	£6.99	$9.95
Venezuela	£8.99	$12.95
Yucatán Peninsula	£6.99	$9.95

Asia	UK RRP	US RRP
Angkor Wat	£5.99	$8.95
Bali & Lombok	£8.99	$12.95
Chennai & Tamil Nadu	£8.99	$12.95
Chiang Mai & Northern Thailand	£7.99	$11.95
Goa	£6.99	$9.95
Hanoi & Northern Vietnam	£8.99	$12.95
Ho Chi Minh City & Mekong Delta	£7.99	$11.95
Java	£7.99	$11.95
Kerala	£7.99	$11.95
Kolkata & West Bengal	£5.99	$8.95
Mumbai & Gujarat	£8.99	$12.95

Africa	UK RRP	US RRP
Beirut	£6.99	$9.95
Damascus	£5.99	$8.95
Durban & KwaZulu Natal	£8.99	$12.95
Fès & Northern Morocco	£8.99	$12.95
Jerusalem	£8.99	$12.95
Johannesburg & Kruger National Park	£7.99	$11.95
Kenya's beaches	£8.99	$12.95
Kilimanjaro & Northern Tanzania	£8.99	$12.95
Zanzibar & Pemba	£7.99	$11.95

Europe	UK RRP	US RRP
Bilbao & Basque Region	£6.99	$9.95
Granada & Sierra Nevada	£6.99	$9.95
Málaga	£5.99	$8.95
Orkney & Shetland Islands	£5.99	$8.95
Skye & Outer Hebrides	£6.99	$9.95

North America	UK RRP	US RRP
Vancouver & Rockies	£8.99	$12.95

Australasia	UK RRP	US RRP
Brisbane & Queensland	£8.99	$12.95
Perth	£7.99	$11.95

For the latest books, e-books and smart phone app releases, and a wealth of travel information, visit us at:
www.footprinttravelguides.com.

footprinttravelguides.com

Join us on facebook for the latest travel news, product releases, offers and amazing competitions: www.facebook.com/footprintbooks.com.